HAL•LEONARD®
GUITAR PLAY-ALONG
SIMPLE STRUMMING SONGS

VOL. 74

AUDIO ACCESS INCLUDED

PLAYBACK+
Speed • Pitch • Balance • Loop

T0081632

CONTENTS

To access audio visit:
www.halleonard.com/mylibrary

Enter Code
1414-8064-1132-0832

ISBN 978-1-4950-4735-0

7777 W. BLUEMOUND RD. P.O. BOX 13819 MILWAUKEE, WI 53213

Visit Hal Leonard Online at
www.halleonard.com

American Pie

Words and Music by Don McLean

Verse

1. Did you ___ write the book of love ___ and do you ___ have faith in
2. *See additional lyrics*

God a - bove, ___ if ___ the Bi - ble tells ___ you so?

Now ___ do you ___ be - lieve ___ in rock 'n' roll? ___ Can

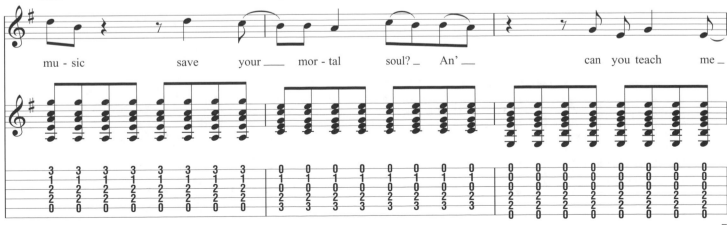

mu - sic save your ___ mor - tal soul? ___ An' ___ can you teach me ___

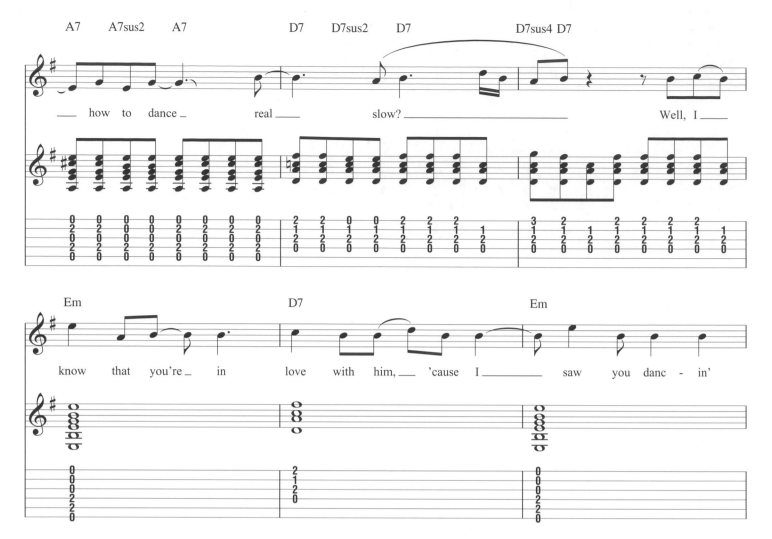

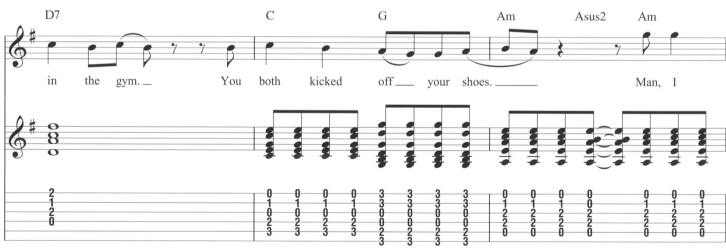

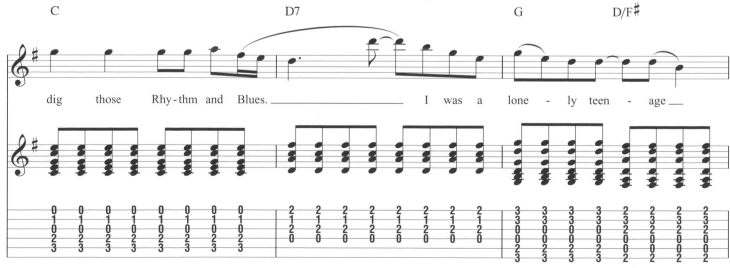

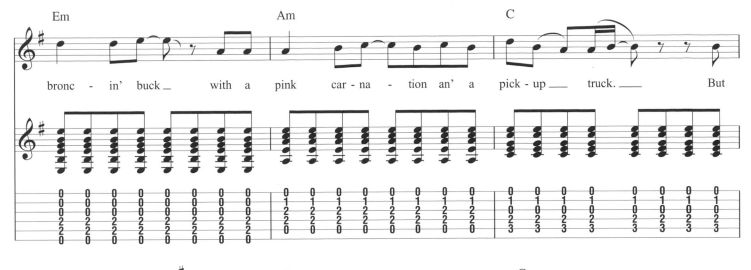

bronc - in' buck __ with a pink car - na - tion an' a pick-up __ truck. __ But

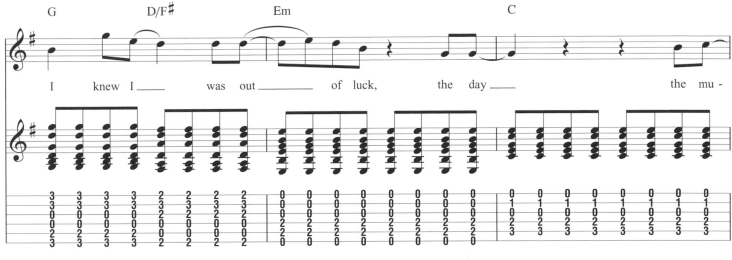

I knew I ___ was out ___ of luck, the day ___ the mu -

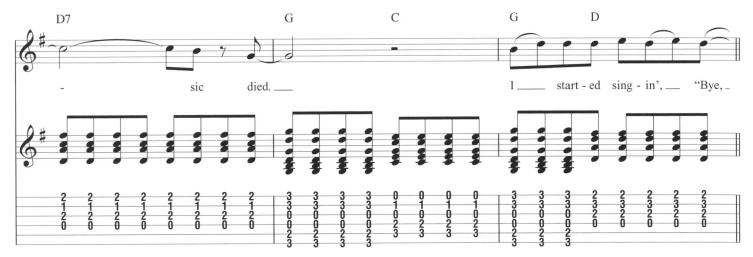

- sic died. ___ I ___ start - ed sing - in', ___ "Bye, __

Chorus

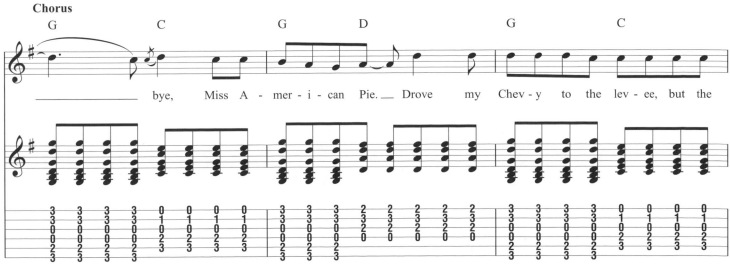

_____ bye, Miss A - mer - i - can Pie. Drove my Chev - y to the lev - ee, but the

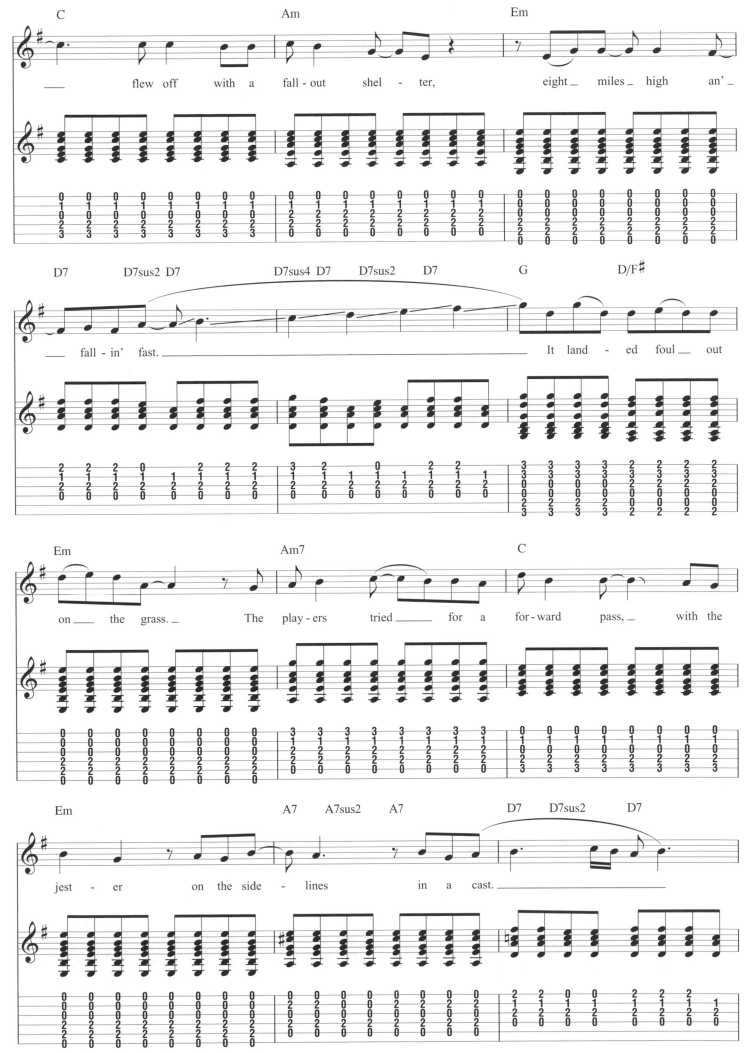

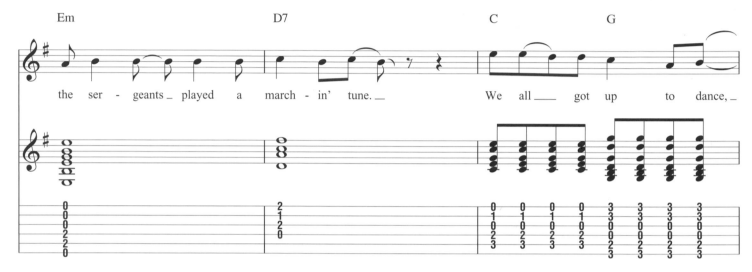

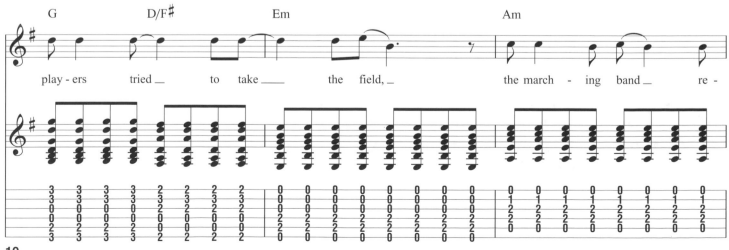

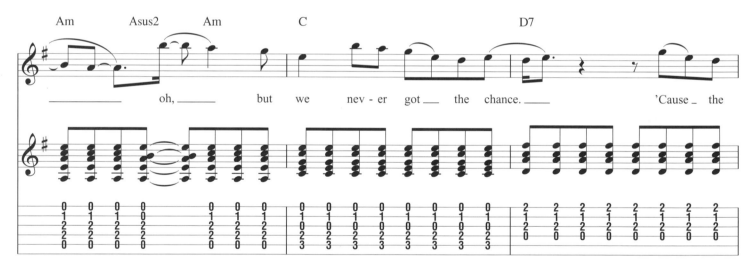

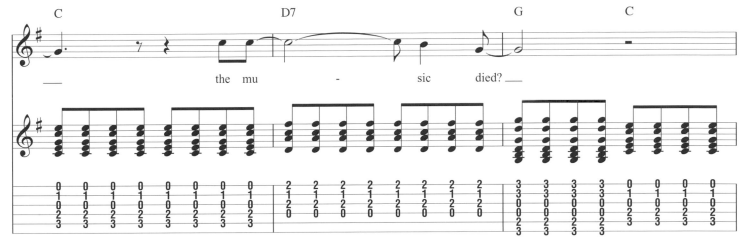

Chorus

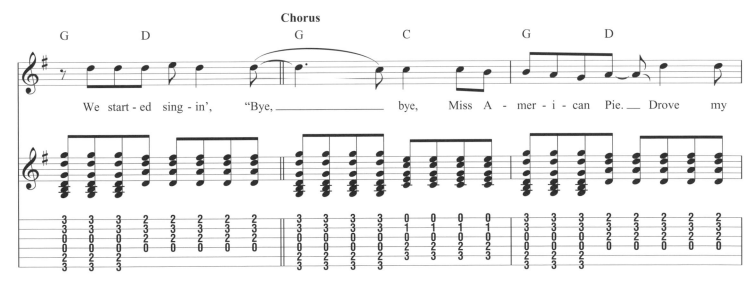

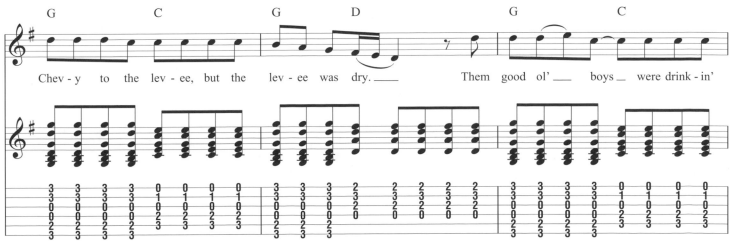

To Coda ⊕

D.S. al Coda

⊕ **Coda**

Verse
Rubato
Half-time feel

Chorus
Moderately slow ♩ = 90

14

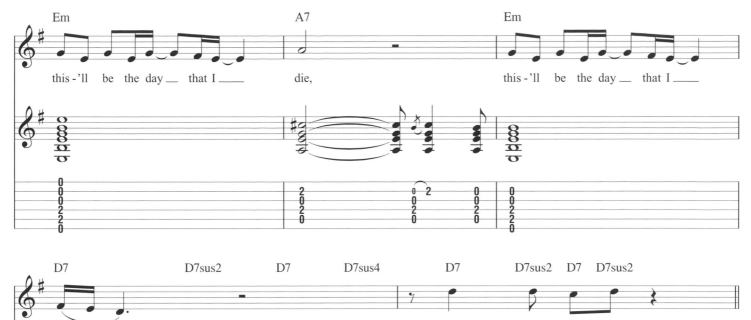

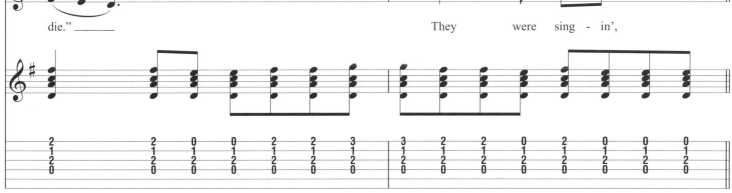

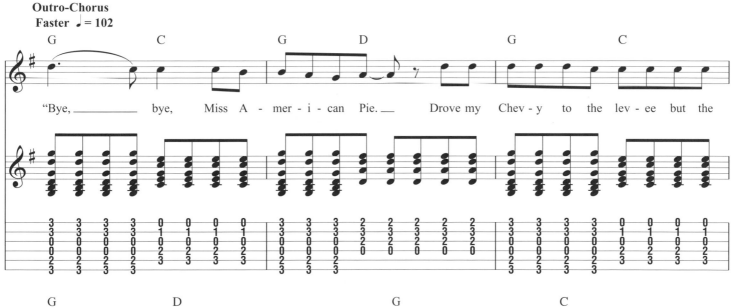

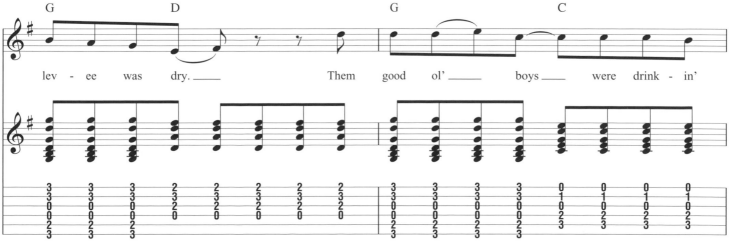

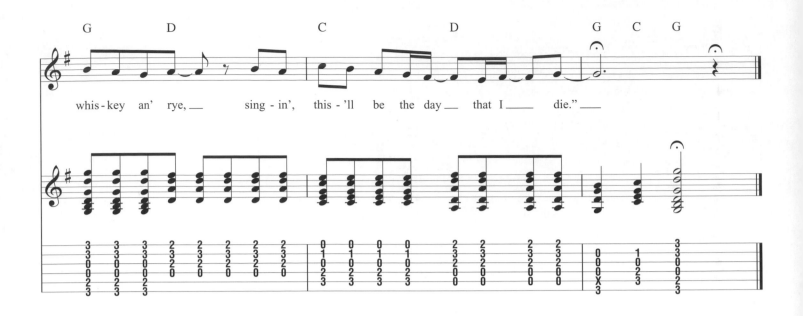

whis-key an' rye, ___ sing-in', this-'ll be the day ___ that I ___ die." ___

Additional Lyrics

2. Now for ten years we've been on our own, and moss grows fat on a rollin' stone.
   But, that's not how it used to be.
   When the jester sang for the king and queen in a coat he borrowed from James Dean,
   And a voice that came from you and me.
   Oh, and while the king was looking down, the jester stole his thorny crown.
   The courtroom was adjourned; no verdict was returned.
   And while Lenin read a book on Marx, the quartet practiced in the park,
   And we sang dirges in the dark the day the music died.
   We were singin',...

4. Oh, and there we were all in one place, a generation lost in space,
   With no time left to start again.
   So come on, Jack be nimble, Jack be quick! Jack Flash sat on a candlestick,
   'Cause fire is the devil's only friend.
   Oh, and as I watched him on the stage, my hands were clenched in fists of rage.
   No angel born in hell could break that Satan's spell.
   And as the flames climbed high into the night to light the sacrificial rite,
   I saw Satan laughing with delight the day the music died.
   He was singin',...

Baby, I Love Your Way

Words and Music by Peter Frampton

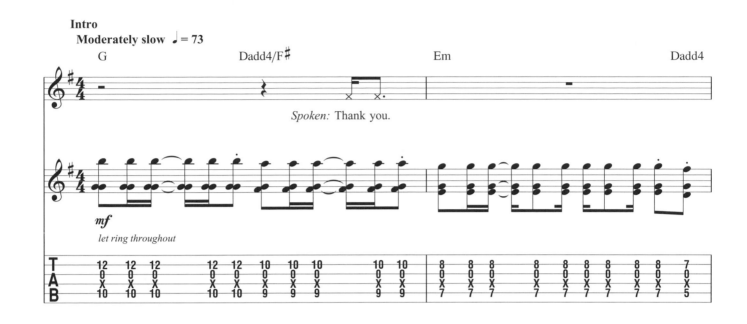

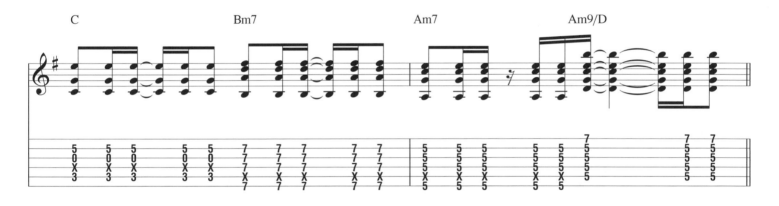

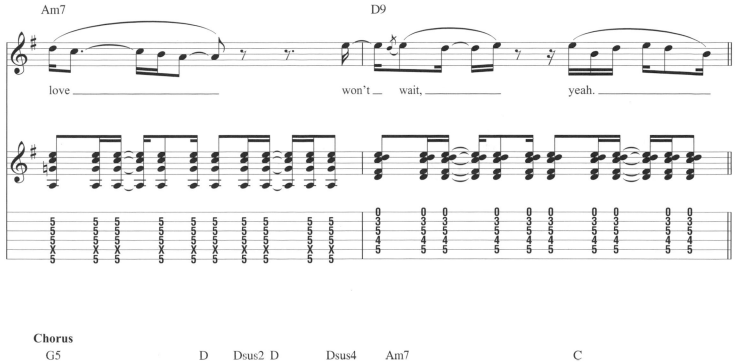

love _____ won't _ wait, _____ yeah. _____

Chorus

Oo, ba - by, I love _ your way, _____ ev -'ry day. _

To Coda 2 ⊕

Want to tell you I love _ your way, _____ ev -'ry day. _

Want to be with you night ___ and day, _____ hey. _____

Interlude

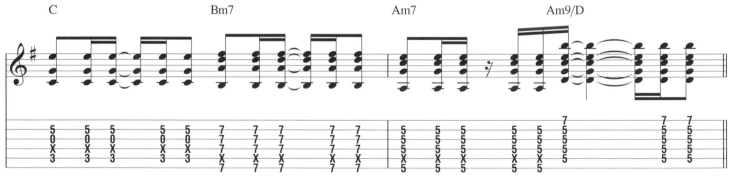

D.S. al Coda 1

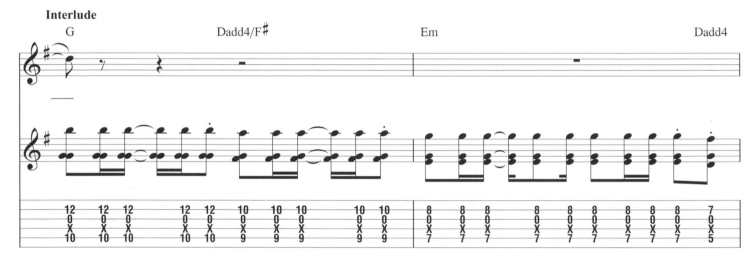

Coda 1

Electric Piano Solo

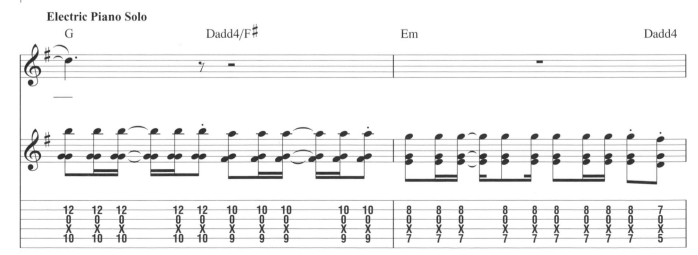

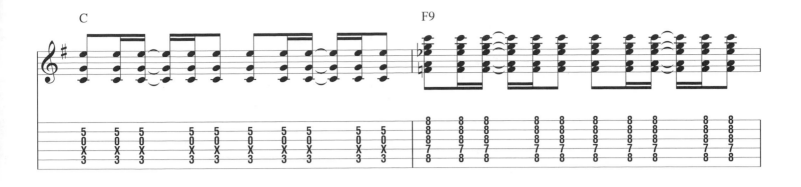

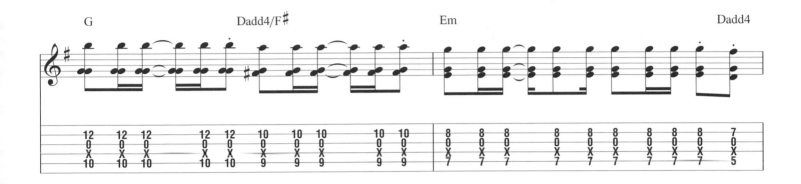

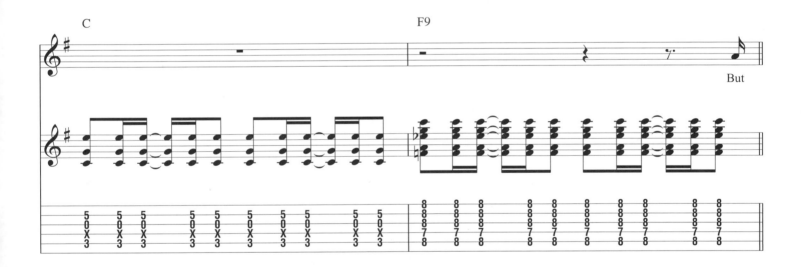

Pre-Chorus

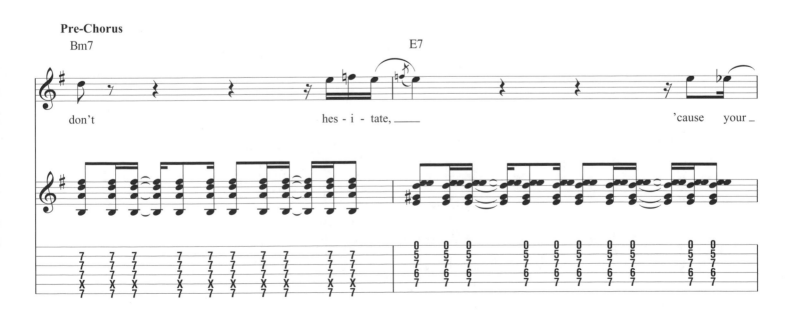

don't   hes - i - tate, ____   'cause your ___

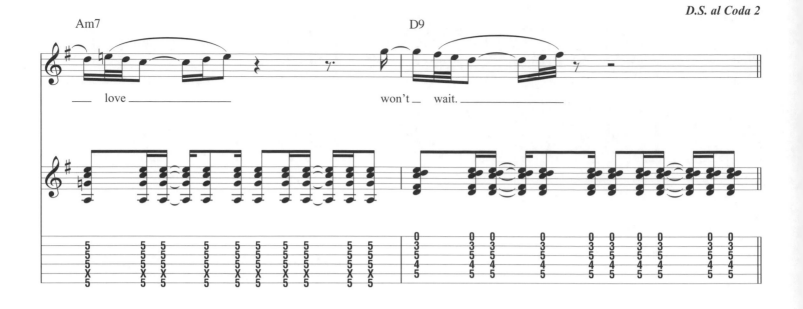

love _____ won't _ wait. _____

 Coda 2

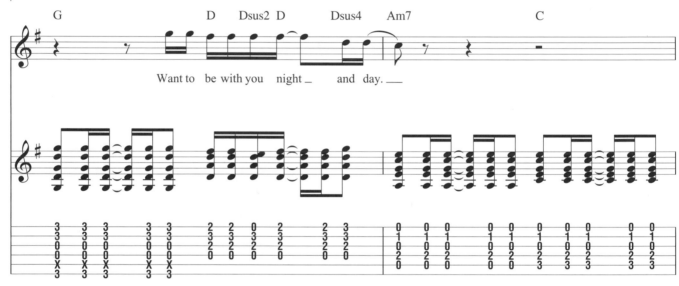

Want to be with you night _ and day. _

Oo, ba - by, I love _ your way, _____ ev -'ry day. _

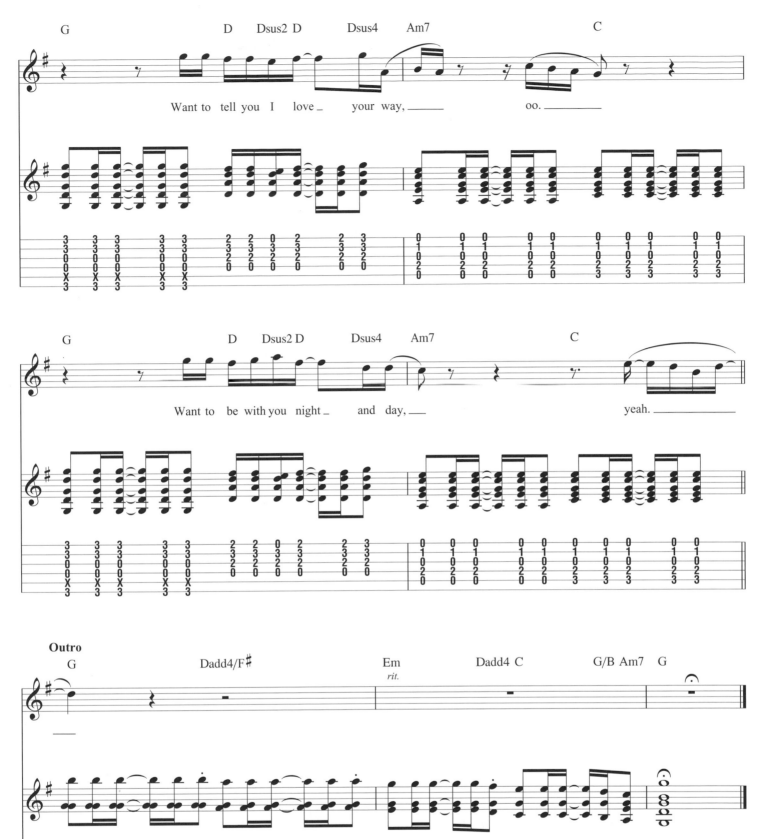

Additional Lyrics

2. Moon appears to shine and light the sky
   With the help of some firefly.
   I wonder how they have the power to shine, shine, shine.
   I can see them under the pine.

3. I can see the sunset in your eyes,
   Brown and grey, and blue besides.
   Clouds are stalking islands in the sun.
   Wish I could buy one out of season.

Barely Breathing

Words and Music by Duncan Sheik

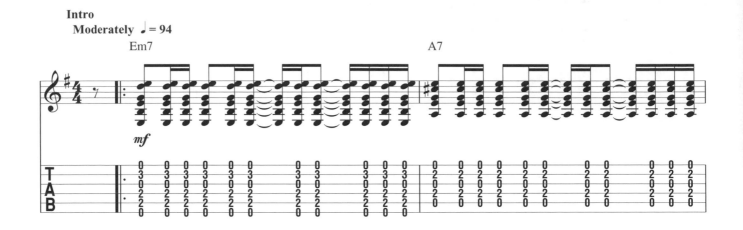

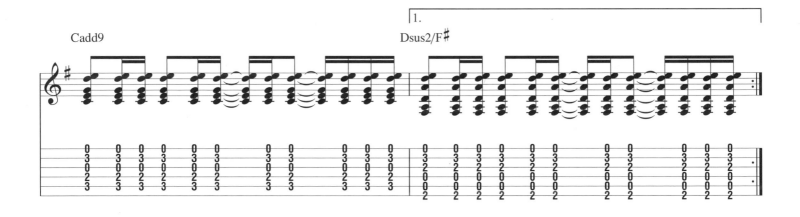

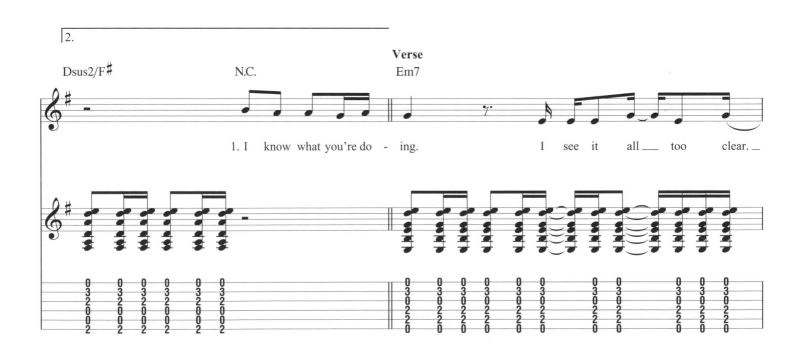

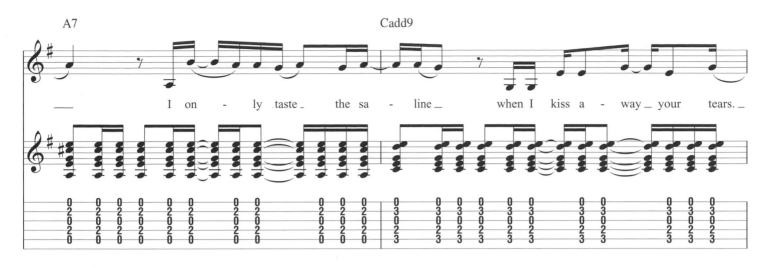

I on - ly taste _ the sa - line _ when I kiss a - way _ your tears. _

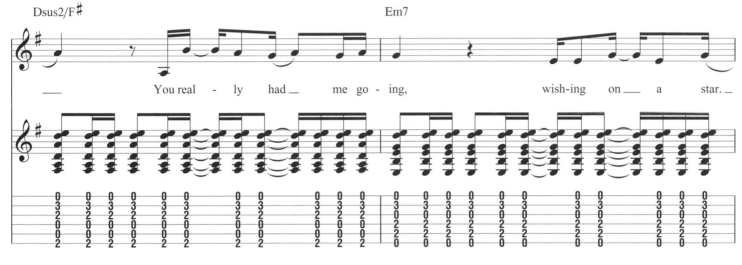

You real - ly had _ me go - ing, wish-ing on _ a star. _

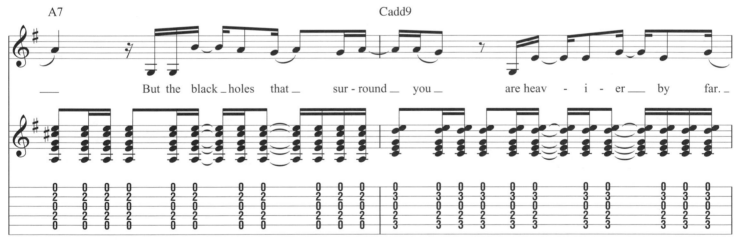

But the black _ holes that _ sur - round _ you _ are heav - i - er _ by far. _

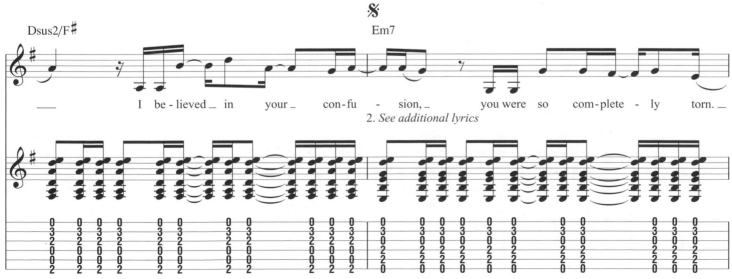

I be - lieved _ in your _ con-fu - sion, _ you were so com-plete - ly torn. _

2. See additional lyrics

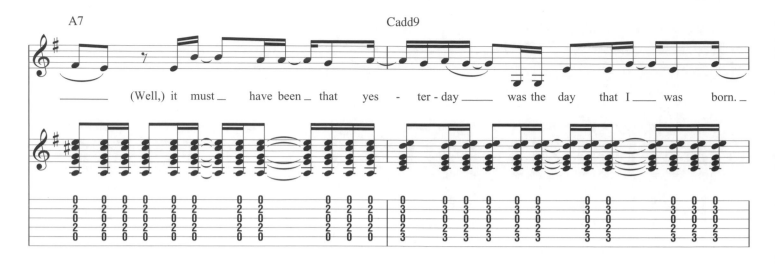

(Well,) it must ___ have been ___ that yes - ter - day ___ was the day that I ___ was born. ___

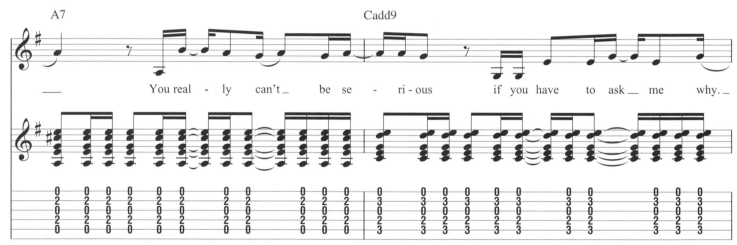

There's not ___ much to ___ ex - am - ine, (there's) noth-ing left ___ to hide. ___

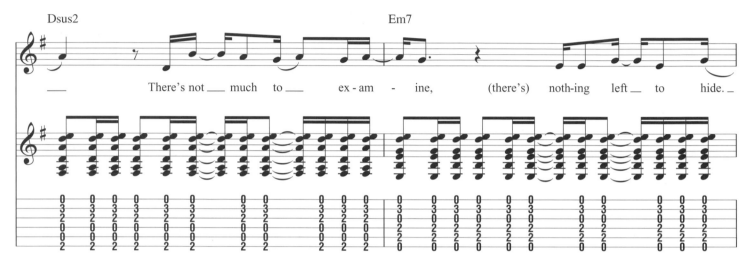

You real - ly can't ___ be se - ri - ous if you have to ask ___ me why. ___

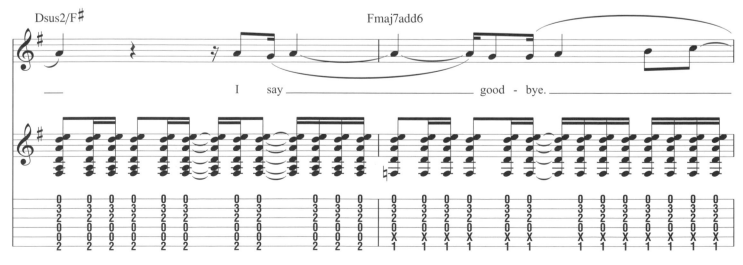

I say ___ good - bye. ___

Chorus

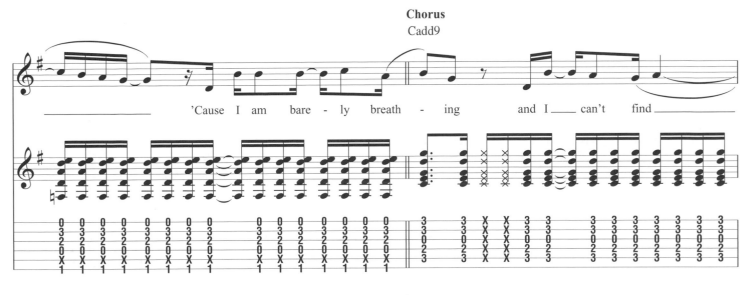

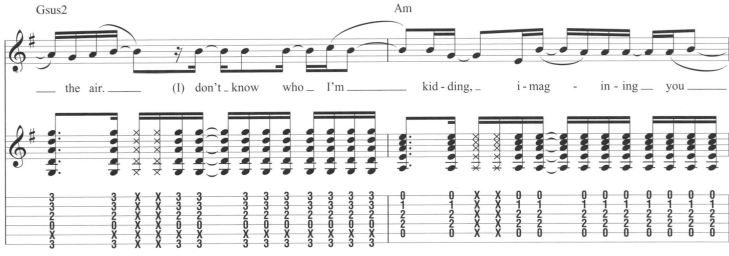

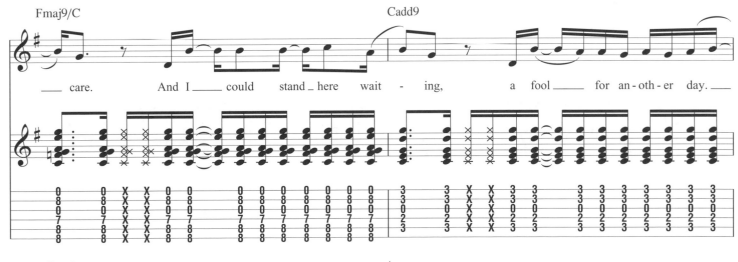

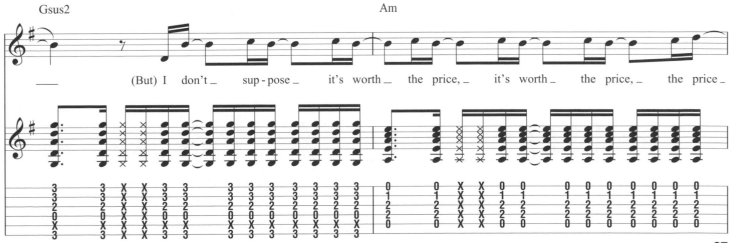

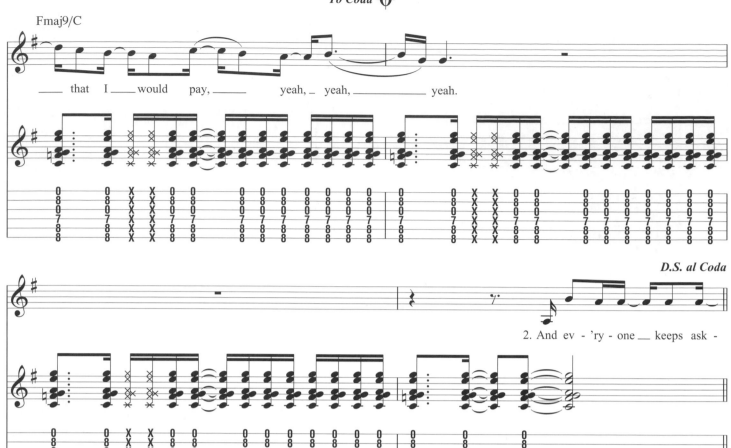

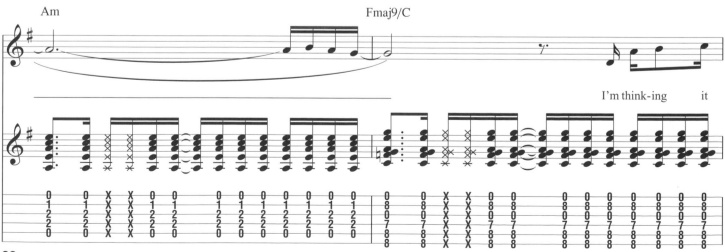

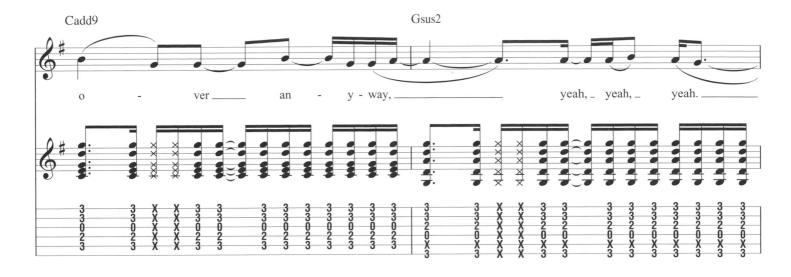

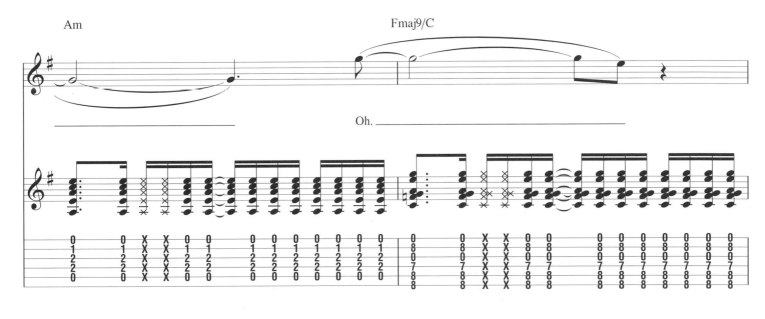

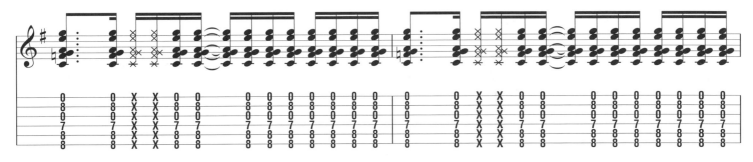

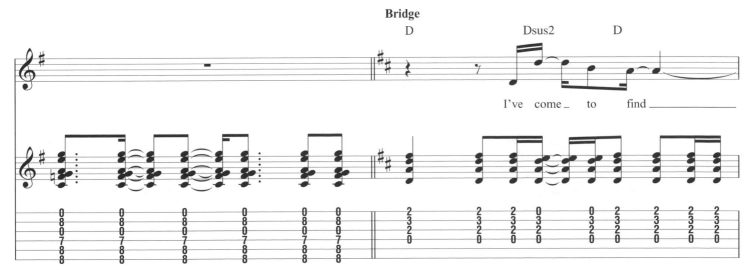

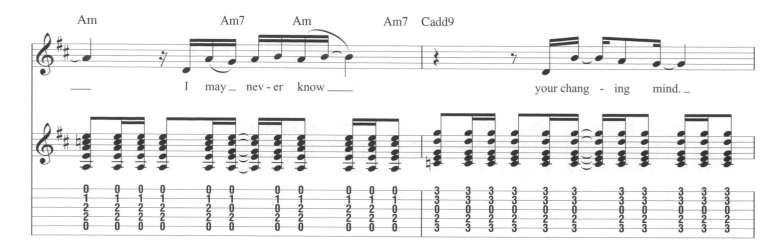

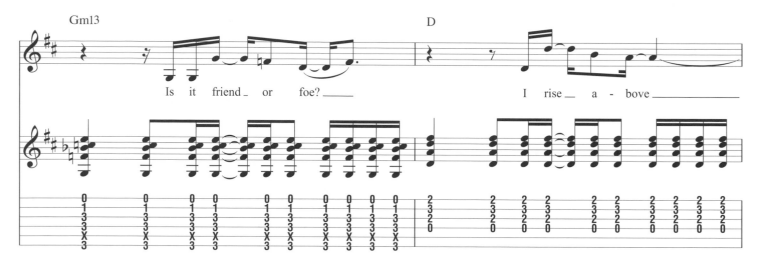

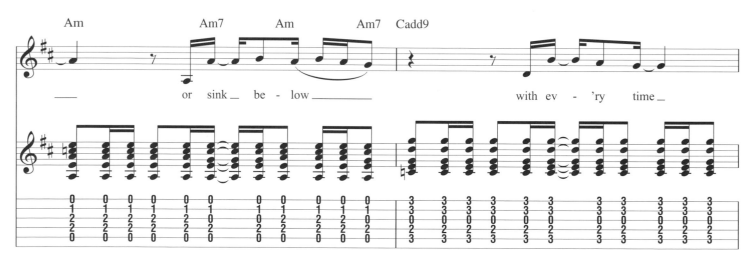

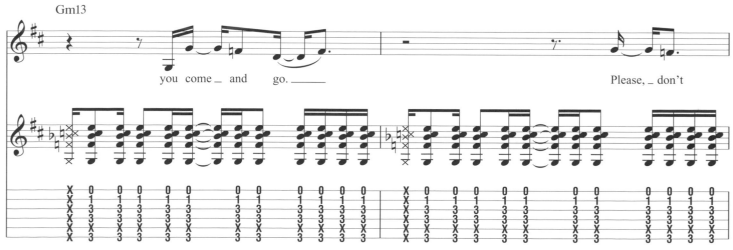

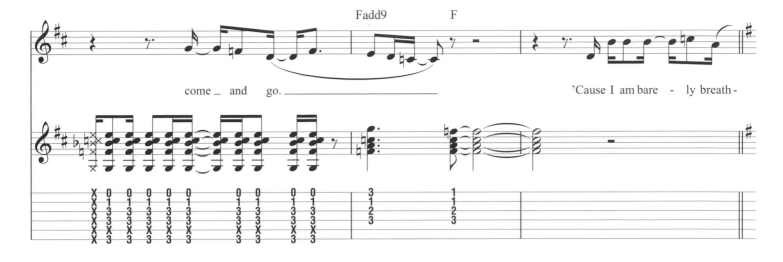

'Cause I am bare - ly breath-

Outro-Chorus

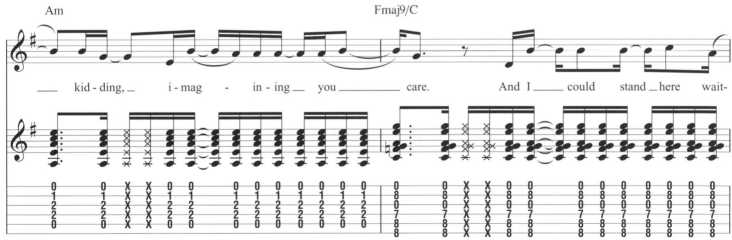

-ing and I ___ can't find ___ the air. ___ (I) don't ___ know who ___ I'm ___

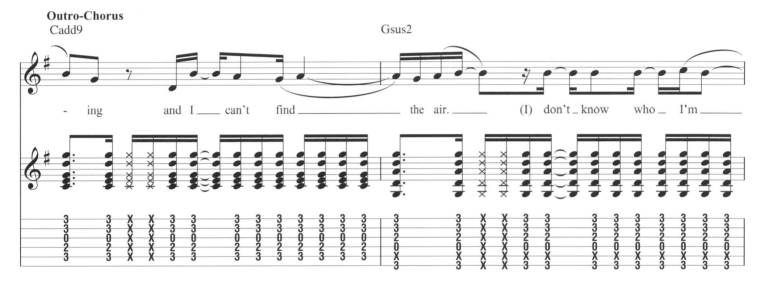

___ kid - ding, ___ i - mag - in - ing ___ you ___ care. And I ___ could stand ___ here wait-

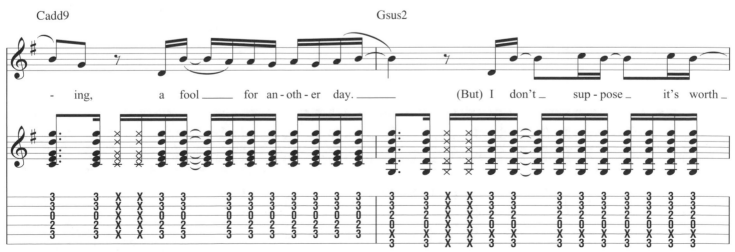

-ing, a fool ___ for an - oth - er day. ___ (But) I don't ___ sup - pose ___ it's worth ___

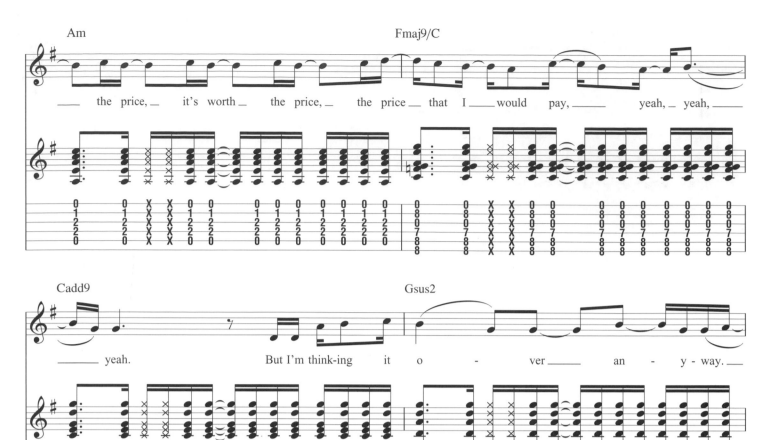

the price, ___ it's worth ___ the price, ___ the price ___ that I ___ would pay, ___ yeah, ___ yeah,

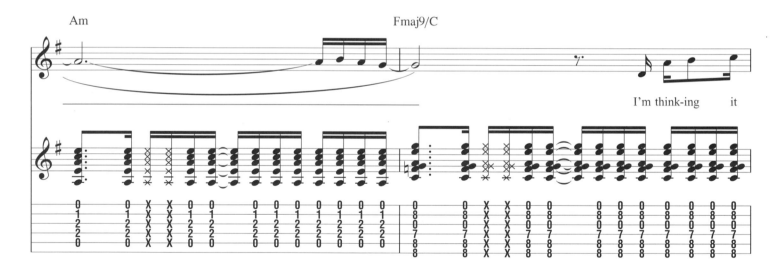

___ yeah. But I'm think-ing it o - ver ___ an - y - way. ___

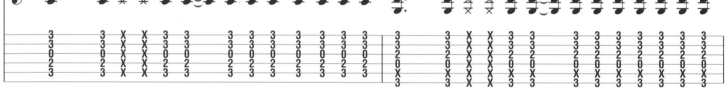

___ I'm think-ing it

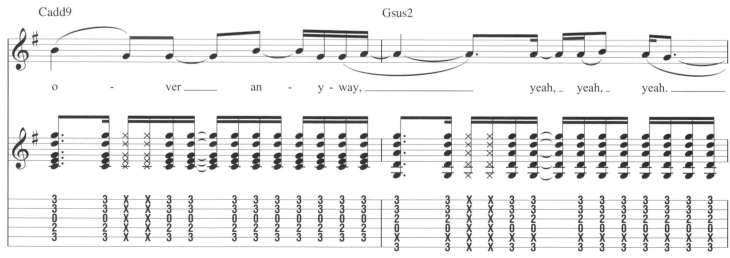

o - ver ___ an - y - way, ___ yeah, ___ yeah, ___ yeah. ___

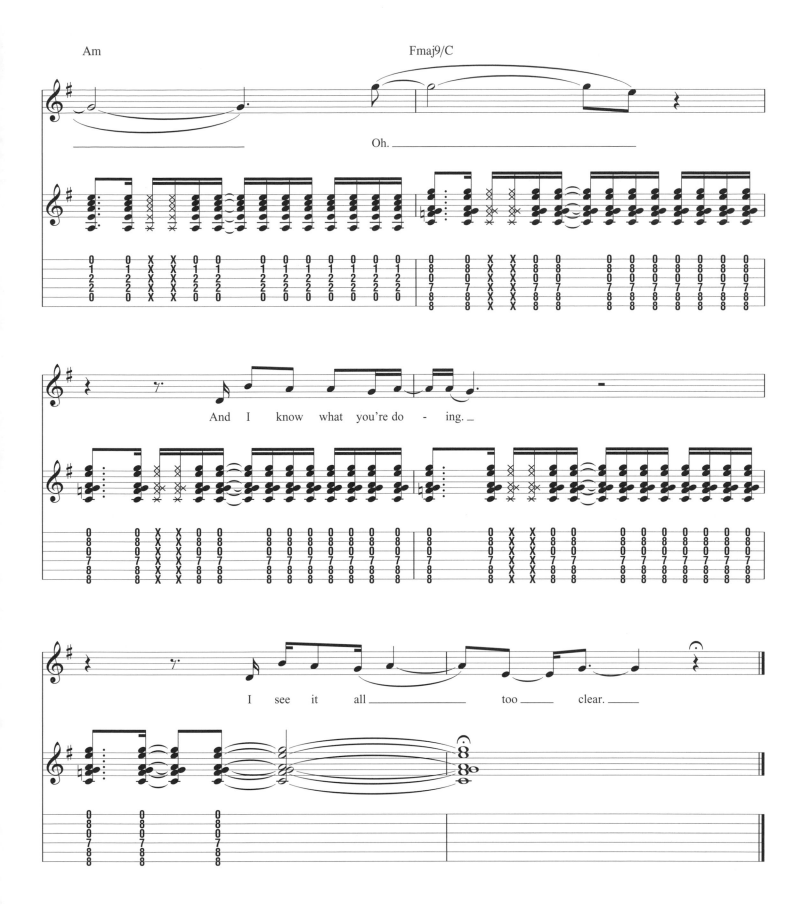

Additional Lyrics

2. And ev'ryone keeps asking, "What's it all about?"
   I used to be so certain; now I can't figure out.
   What is this attraction? I only feel the pain.
   And nothing left to reason, and only you to blame.
   Will it ever change?

Boulevard of Broken Dreams

Words by Billie Joe
Music by Green Day

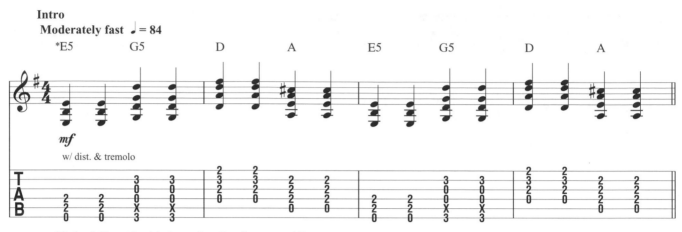

Intro
Moderately fast ♩ = 84

*Optional: To match original recording, Capo I or tune up 1/2 step.

Verse

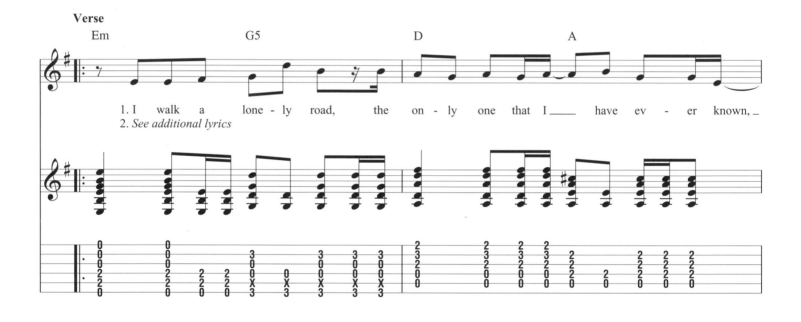

1. I walk a lone-ly road, the on-ly one that I ___ have ev - er known, ___
2. *See additional lyrics*

___ Don't know where it goes, but it's home to me ___ and I walk a - lone. ___

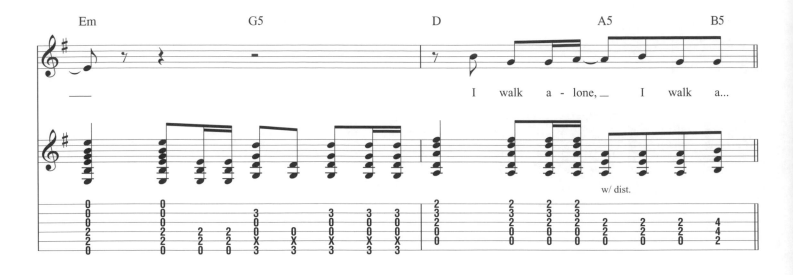

Em   G5   D   A5   B5

I walk a - lone, __ I walk a...

w/ dist.

𝄋 Chorus

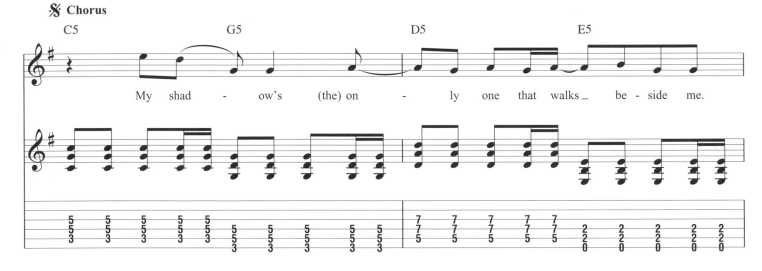

C5   G5   D5   E5

My shad - ow's (the) on - ly one that walks __ be - side me.

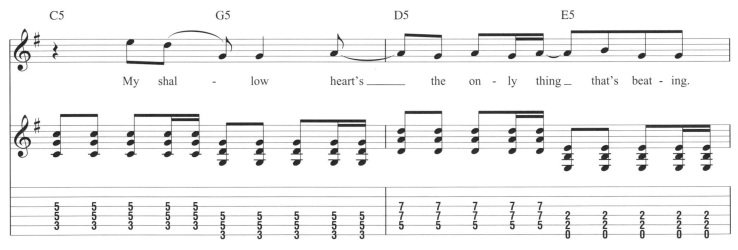

C5   G5   D5   E5

My shal - low heart's _____ the on - ly thing __ that's beat - ing.

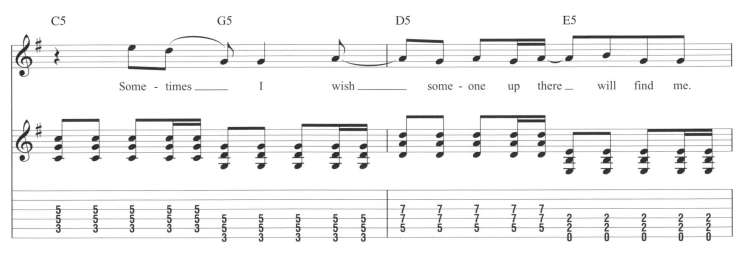

C5   G5   D5   E5

Some - times _____ I wish _____ some - one up there __ will find me.

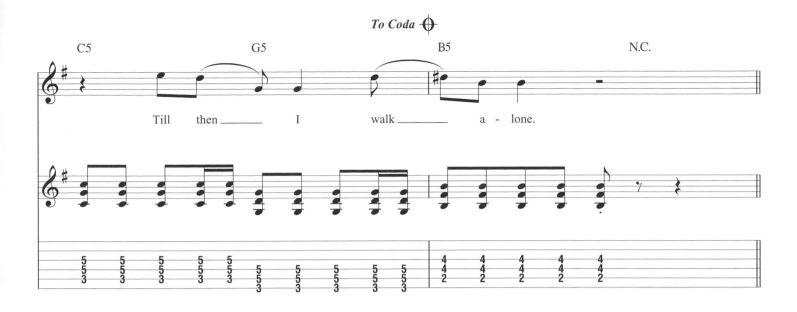

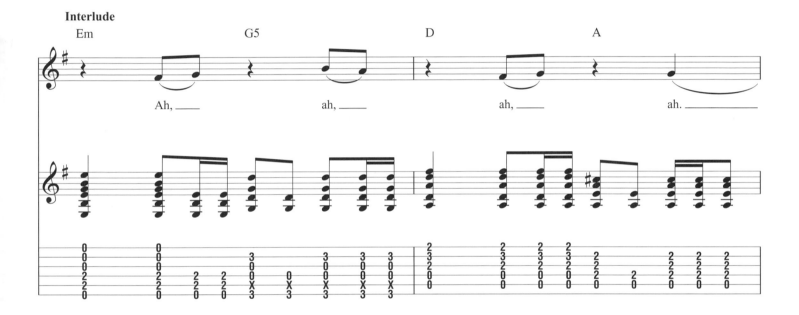

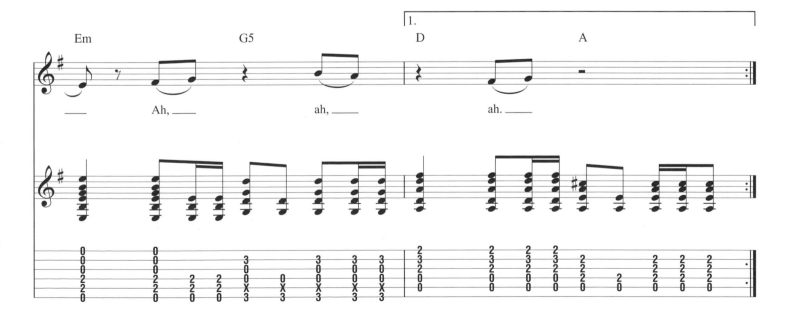

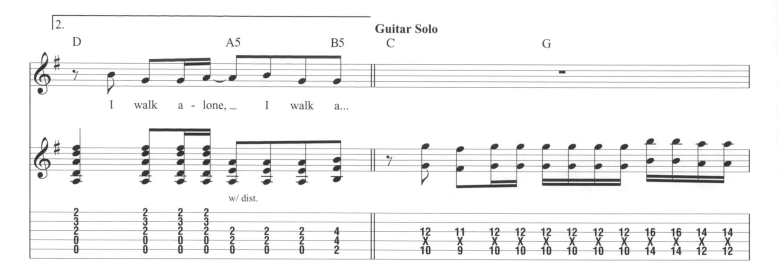

I walk a - lone, __ I walk a...

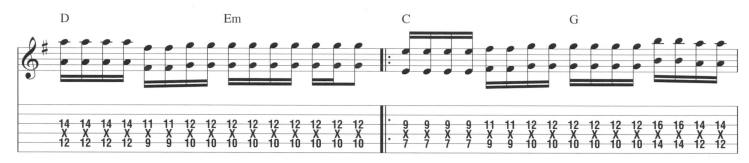

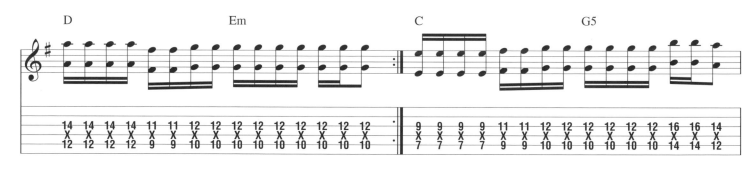

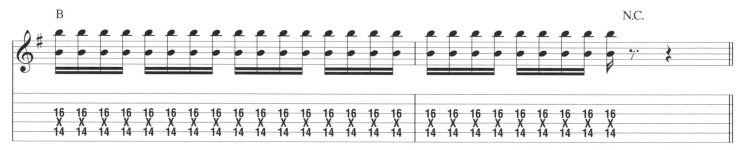

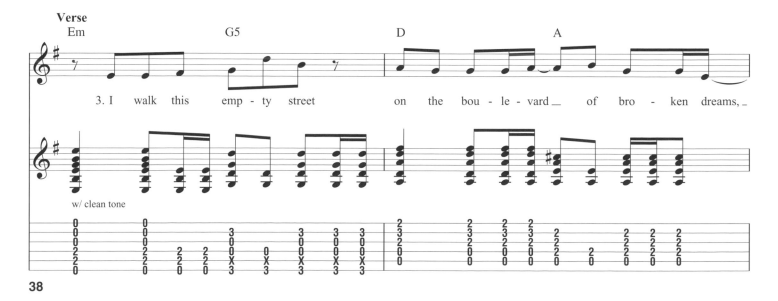

3. I walk this emp - ty street on the bou - le - vard __ of bro - ken dreams, __

when the cit-y sleeps and I'm the on-ly one ___ and I walk a...

w/ dist.

Coda

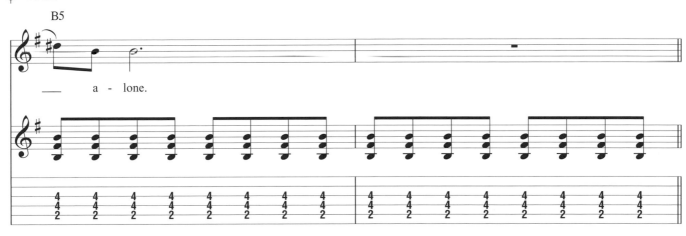

___ a - lone.

Outro

Play 3 times

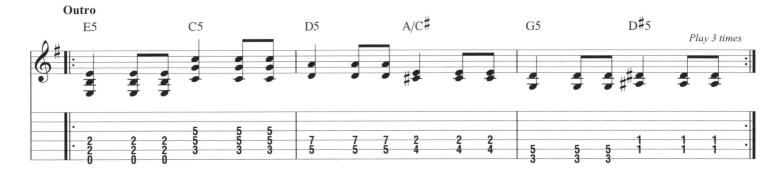

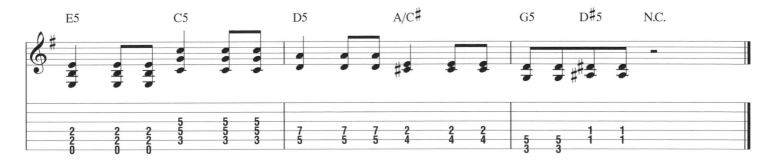

Additional Lyrics

2. I'm walkin' down the line that divides me somewhere in my mind.
On the borderline of the edge and where I walk alone.
Read between the lines, what's fucked up and ev'rything's alright.
Check my vital signs to know I'm still alive and I walk alone.
I walk alone, I walk alone.
I walk alone, I walk a...

Chasing Cars

Words and Music by Gary Lightbody, Tom Simpson, Paul Wilson, Jonathan Quinn and Nathan Connolly

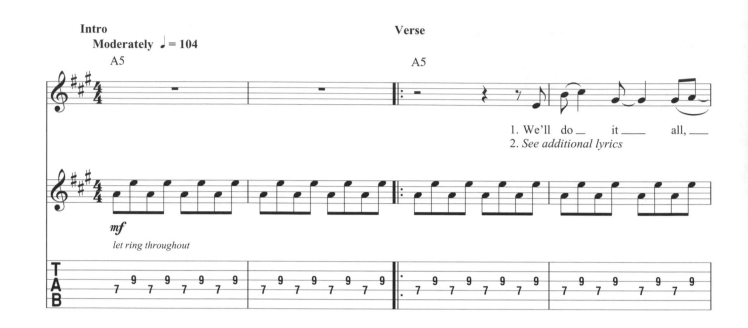

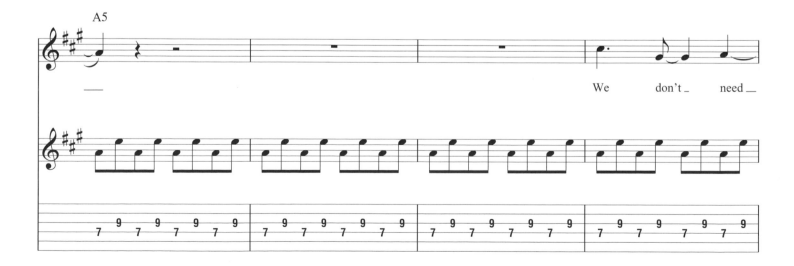

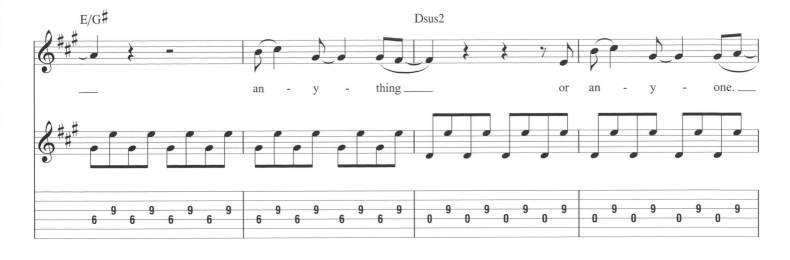

an - y - thing _____ or an - y - one. _____

𝄋 Chorus

_____ If I lay here, if I just

*3rd time, w/ dist.

lay here, _ would you lie with me _ and just for - get the world?

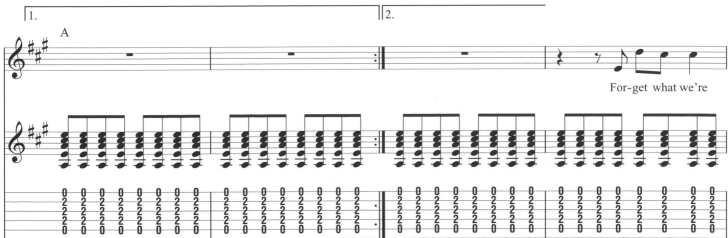

1. 2.

For-get what we're

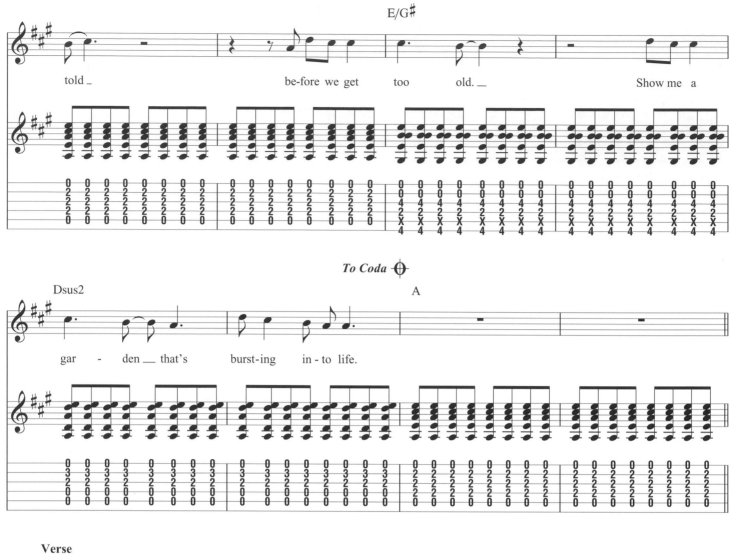

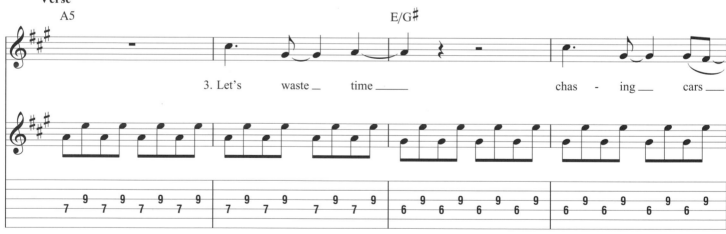

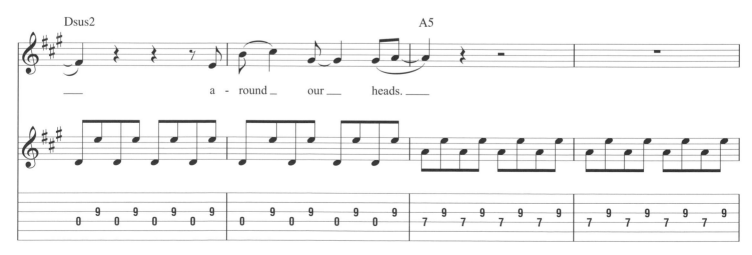

E/G#

I need _ your _ grace _____ to re - mind _ me _____

D.S. al Coda
(take 2nd ending)

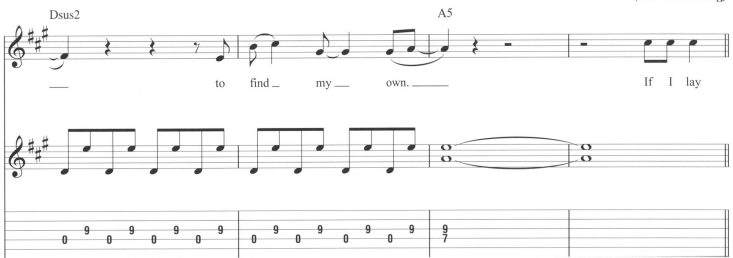

Dsus2   A5

_ to find _ my _ own. _____ If I lay

⊕ **Coda**

A

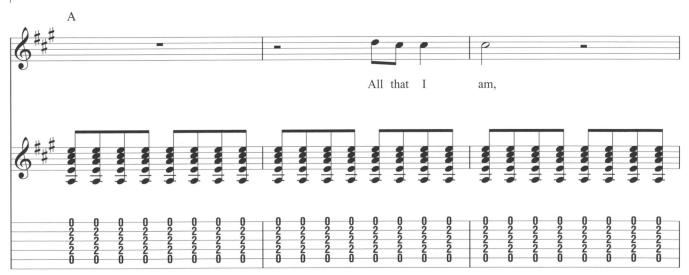

All that I am,

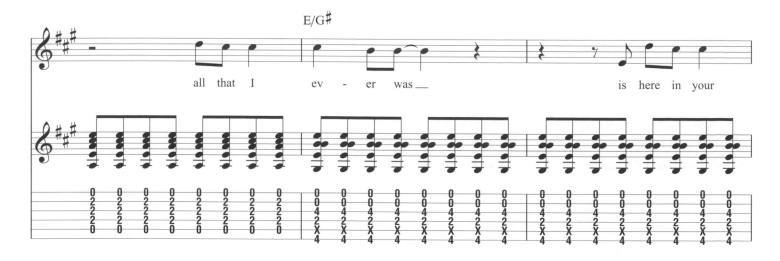

E/G#

all that I ev - er was ___ is here in your

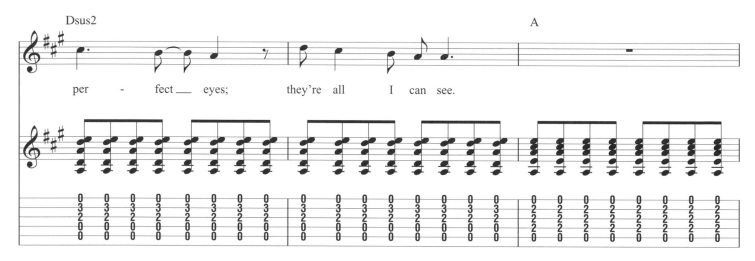

Dsus2   A

per - fect ___ eyes; they're all I can see.

I don't know where,   con-fused a - bout

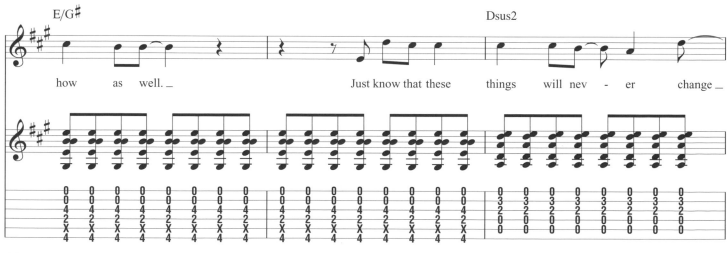

E/G#   Dsus2

how as well. ___   Just know that these things will nev - er change ___

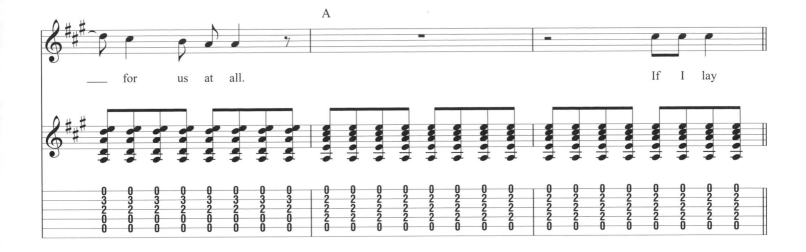

for us at all.   If I lay

Outro

here,   if I just   lay   here, __   would you lie

with   me __ and   just for - get the world?

Additional Lyrics

2. I don't quite know how to say how I feel.
   Those three words are said too much. They're not enough.

Drops of Jupiter
(Tell Me)

**Words and Music by Pat Monahan, James Stafford,
Robert Hotchkiss, Charles Colin and Scott Underwood**

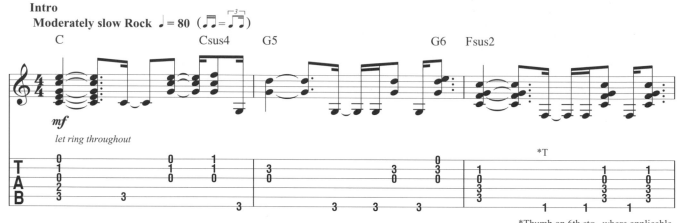

Pre-Chorus

tell me, did you sail a - cross the sun? Did you make it to the Milk - y Way

to see the lights all fad - ed, and that heav - en is o - ver - rat - ed?

Tell me, did you fall from a shoot - ing star, one with - out a per - ma - nent

scar, and did you miss me while you were look - in' for your - self out there?

48

Chorus

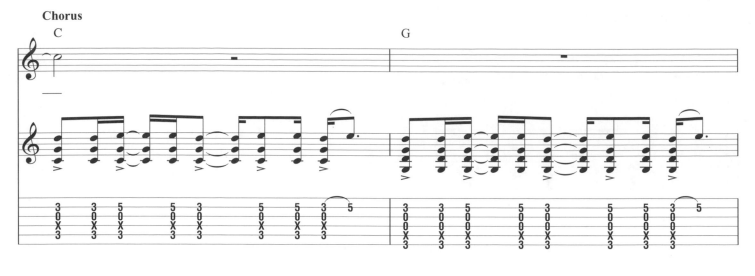

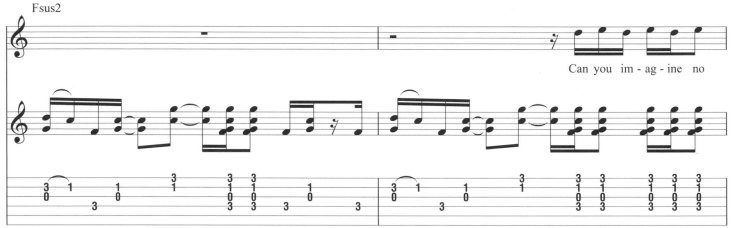

Can you im - ag - ine no

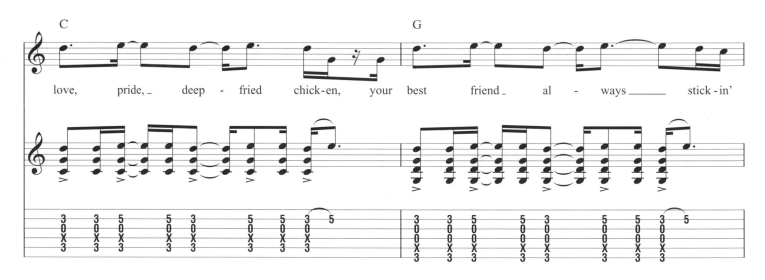

love, pride, __ deep - fried chick - en, your best friend __ al - ways ____ stick - in'

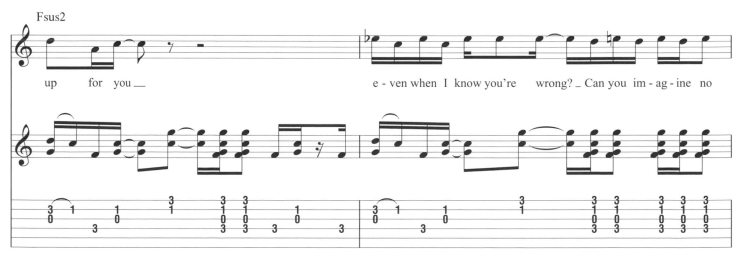

up for you __   e - ven when I know you're wrong? _ Can you im - ag - ine no

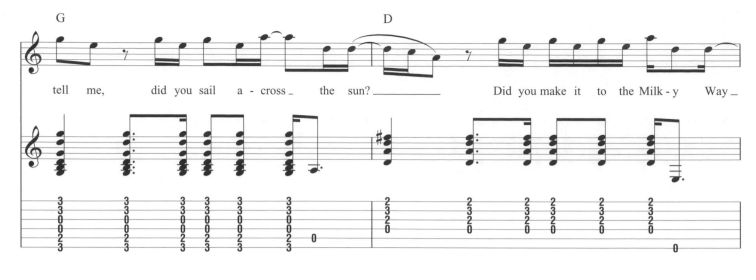

tell me, did you sail a-cross_ the sun?_____ Did you make it to the Milk-y Way_

__ to see_ the lights_ all fad — ed, __ and that heav-en is o - ver-rat - ed? And

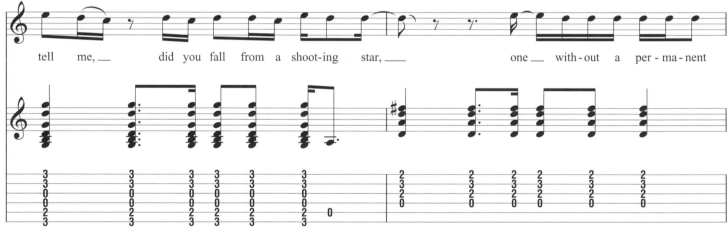

tell me, __ did you fall from a shoot-ing star, __ one __ with-out a per - ma - nent

scar, and did__ you__ miss__ me __ while_ you were look - in' for __ your - self?

Outro-Chorus

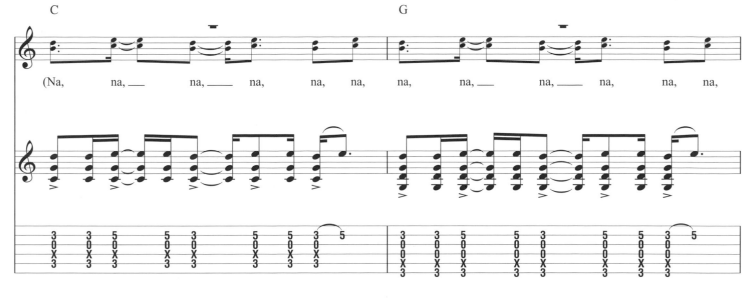

(Na, na, na, na, na, na, na, na, na, na, na, na,

And did you fin-'ly get the chance to dance along the light of day?

na, na.

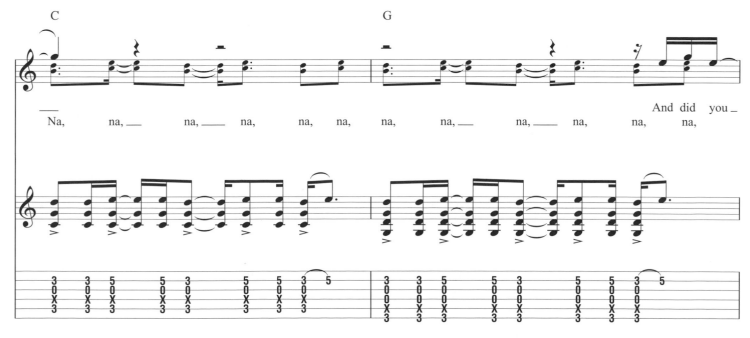

Na, na, na, na, na, na, na, na, na, na, na, na, And did you

Fsus2

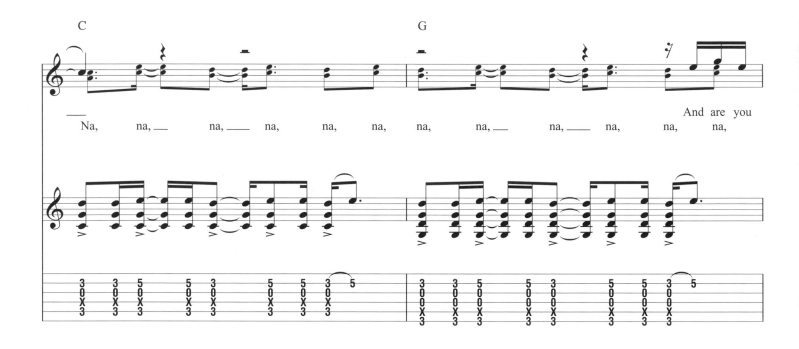

____ fall _____ from a shoot-ing star, _____ fall _____ from a shoot-ing star? _____
na, _____ na.

C   G

____
Na,   na, ___ na, ___ na,   na,   na,   na,   na,   na, ___ na, ___ na,   na,

And are you

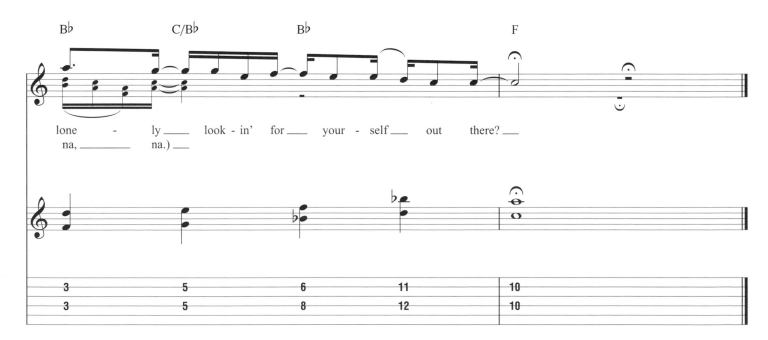

B♭   C/B♭   B♭   F

lone - ly ____ look - in' for ____ your-self ____ out   there? ____
na, _____ na.) ____

Hey Jude

Words and Music by John Lennon and Paul McCartney

*Symbols in parentheses represent chord names respective to capoed guitar.
Symbols above reflect actual sounding chords. Capoed fret is "0" in tab.

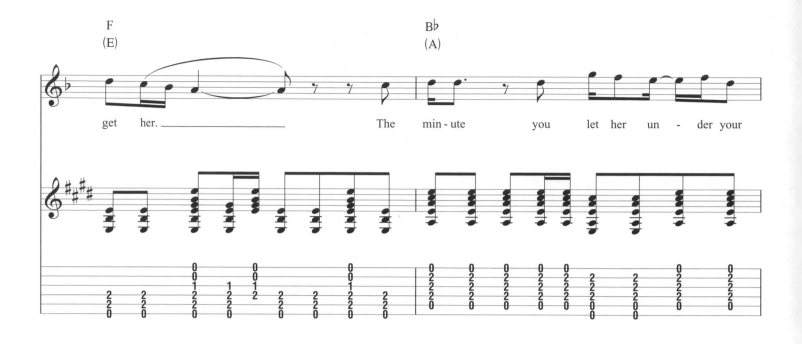

get her._____ The min - ute you let her un - der your

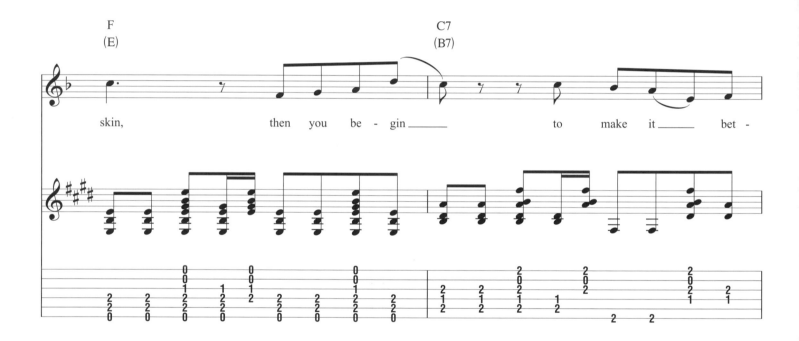

skin, then you be - gin_____ to make it _____ bet -

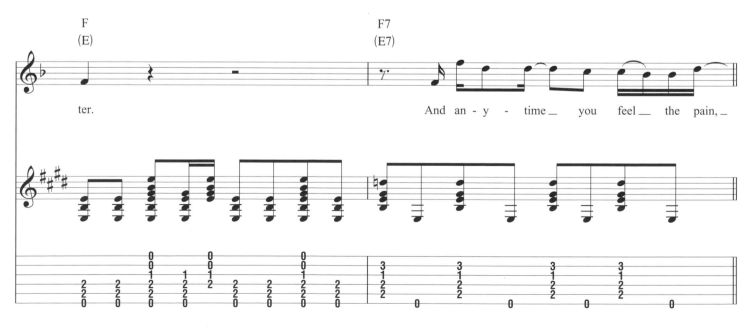

ter. And an - y - time __ you feel __ the pain, __

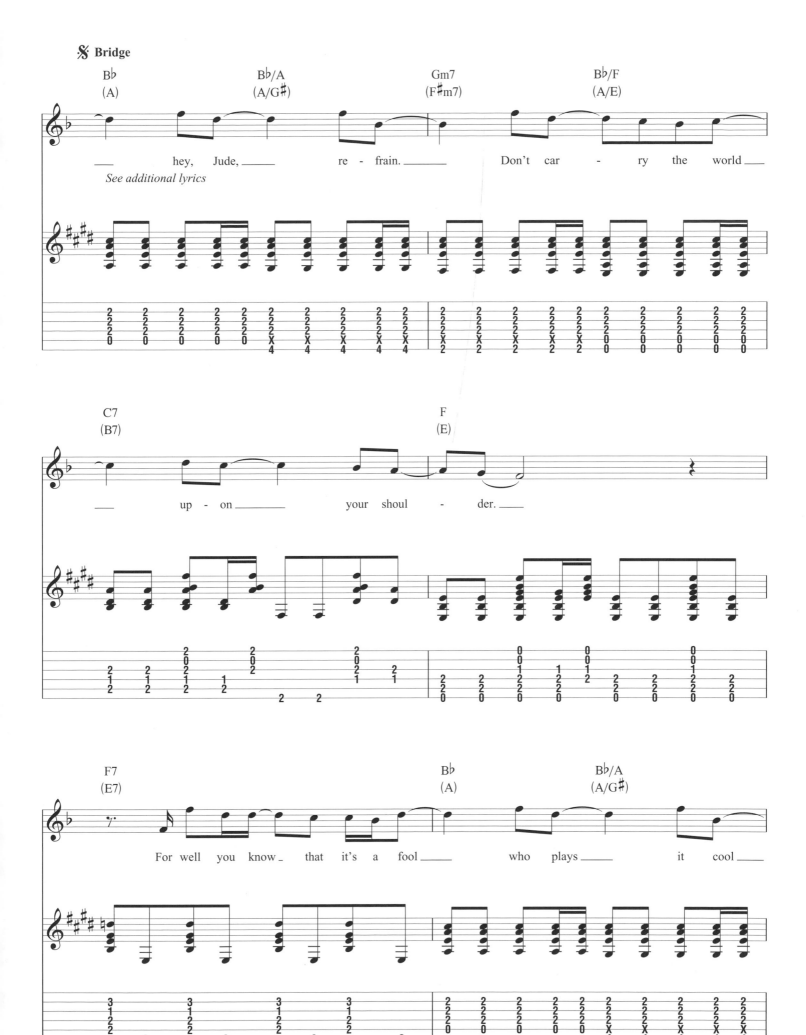

§ **Bridge**

See additional lyrics

__ hey, Jude, _____ re - frain. _____ Don't car - ry the world _____

__ up - on _____ your shoul - der. _____

For well you know_ that it's a fool _____ who plays _____ it cool _____

To Coda ⊕

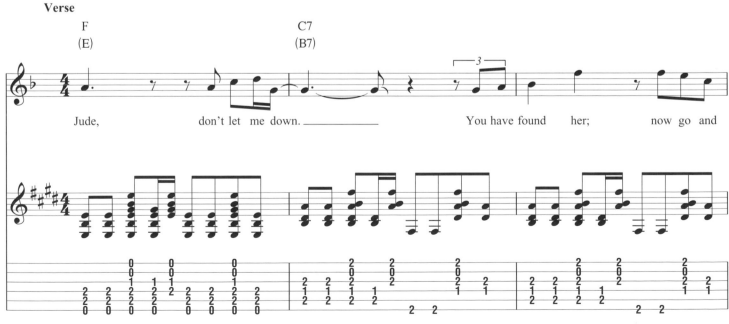

Verse

60

D.S. al Coda

Coda

Outro

Repeat and fade

Additional Lyrics

Bridge So let it out and let it in.
Hey, Jude, begin.
You're waiting for someone to perform with.
And don't you know that it's just you?
Hey, Jude, you'll do.
The movement you need is on your shoulder.
Na, na, na, na, na, na, na, na, na.

Half of My Heart

Words and Music by John Mayer

Capo I

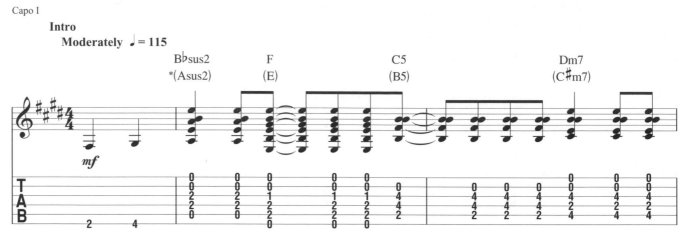

*Symbols in parentheses represent chord names respective to capoed guitar.
Symbols above reflect actual sounding chords. Capoed fret is "0" in tab.

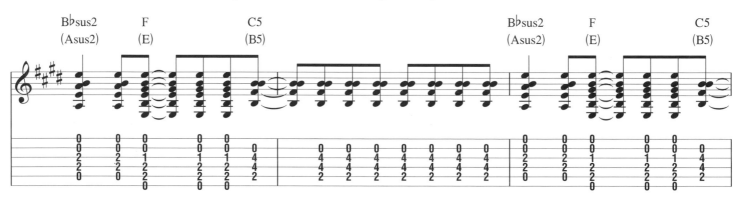

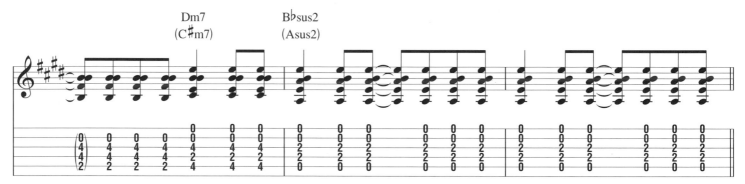

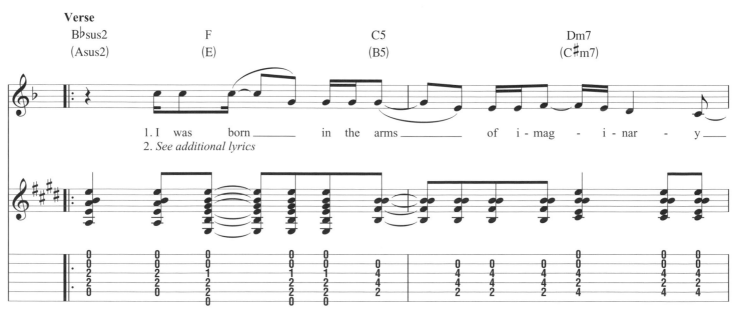

1. I was born _____ in the arms _____ of i-mag-i-nar-y _____
2. *See additional lyrics*

hate that I nev-er gave more to you __ than __ half of my heart, ____

but I can't stop __ lov-ing you. (I can't stop lov-ing you.

can't stop __ lov-ing you. I can't stop lov-ing you.) I can't stop __ lov-ing you __

Additional Lyrics

2. I was made to believe I'd never love somebody else.
   Made a plan, stay the man who can only love himself.

Pre-Chorus Lonely was the song I sang till the day you came.
   Showing me another way, and all that my love can bring.

A Horse with No Name

Words and Music by Dewey Bunnell

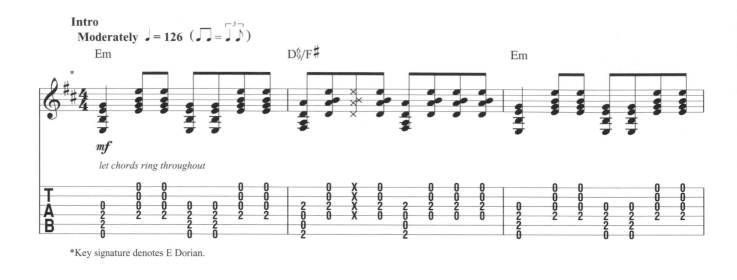

*Key signature denotes E Dorian.

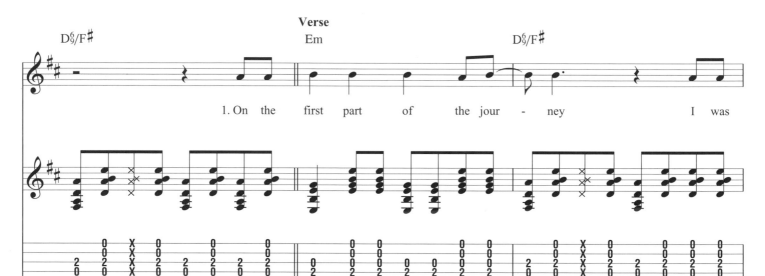

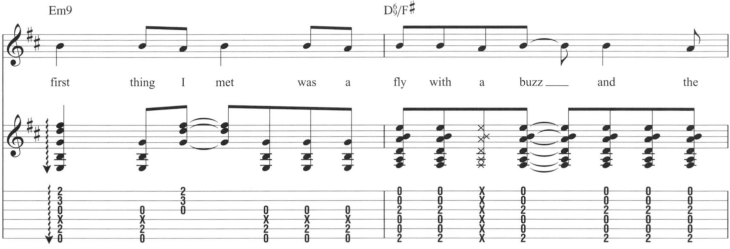

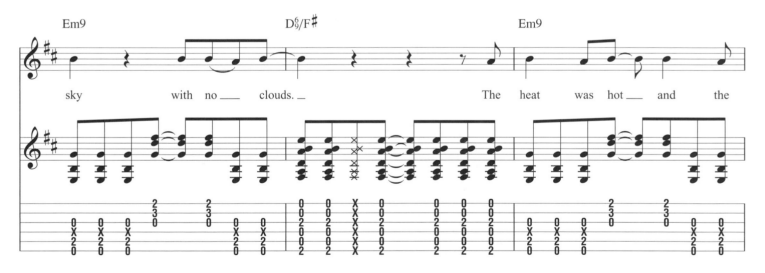

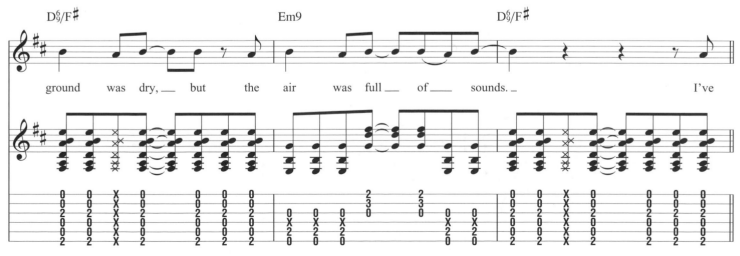

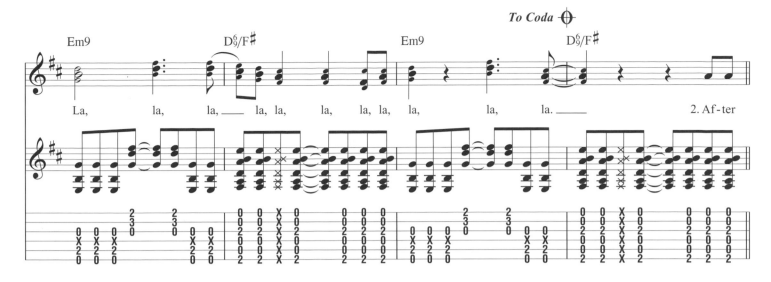

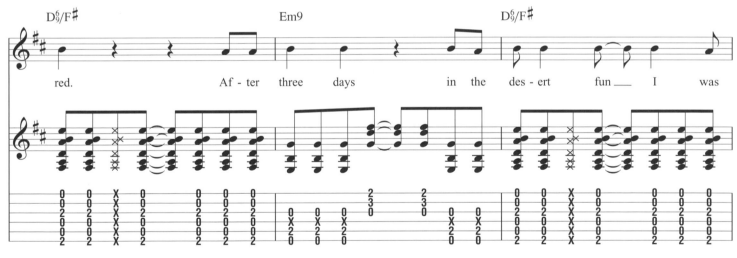

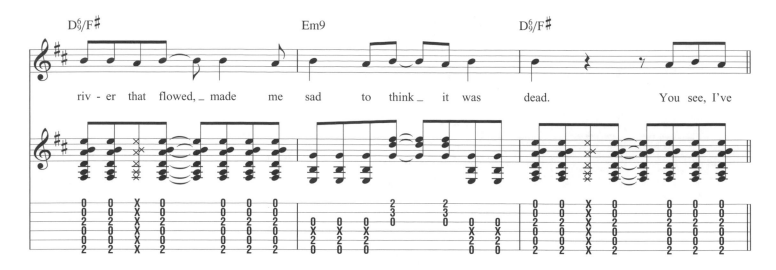

riv - er that flowed, _ made me sad to think _ it was dead. You see, I've

Chorus

been through the des - ert on a horse with no name. _ It felt good to be out of the

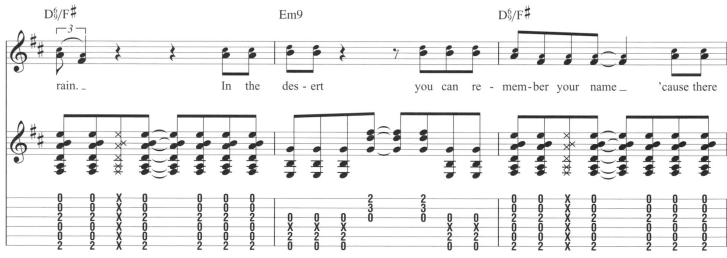

rain. _ In the des - ert you can re - mem - ber your name _ 'cause there

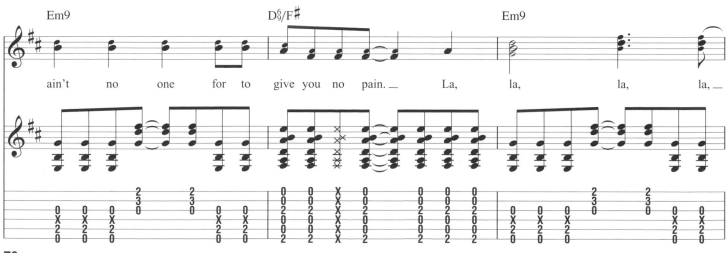

ain't no one for to give you no pain. _ La, la, la, la,

la, la, la, la, la, la, la, la. ____ La,

la, la, la, ____ la, la, la, la, la, la, la, la. ____

Guitar Solo

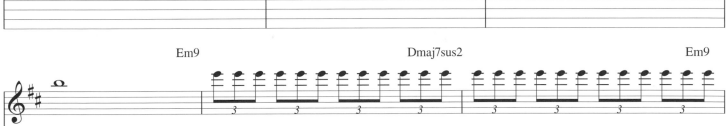

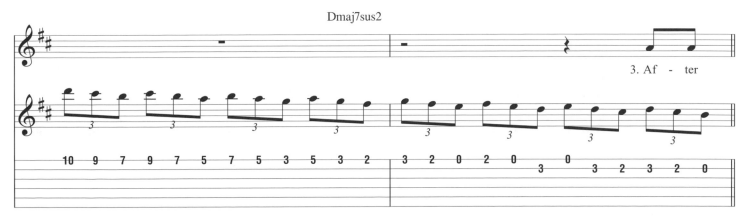

3. Af - ter

Verse

nine days I let the horse run ___ free ___ 'cause the des - ert had turned ___ to ___ sea. ___

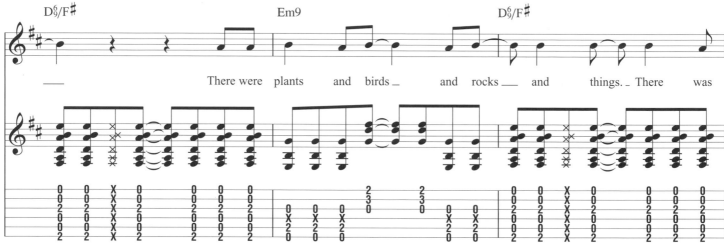

___ There were plants and birds ___ and rocks ___ and things. _ There was

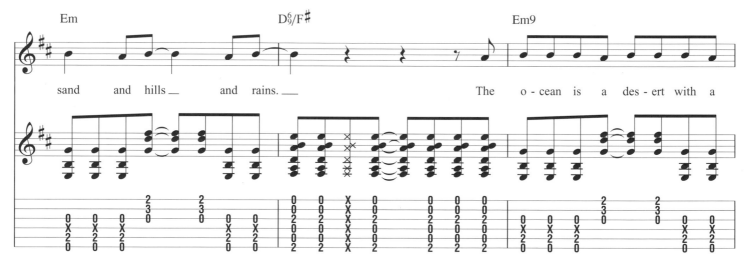

sand and hills ___ and rains. ___ The o - cean is a des - ert with a

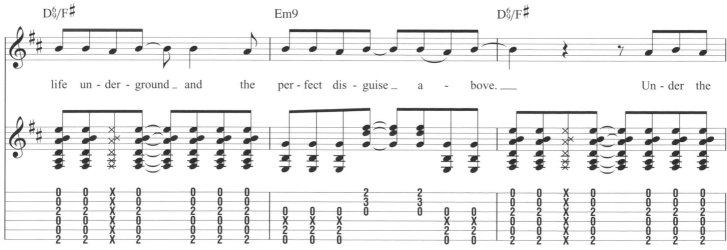

life un - der - ground ___ and the per - fect dis - guise ___ a - bove. ___ Un - der the

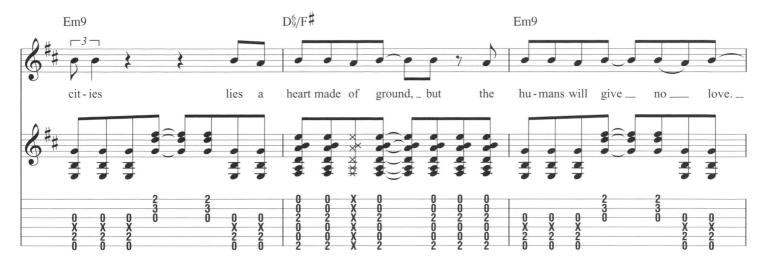

cit-ies   lies a heart made of ground, _ but   the   hu-mans will give _ no _ love. _

D.S. al Coda   ⊕ **Coda**   **Outro**

_ You see I've   _ La,   la,   la,   la, _
                                                   La,

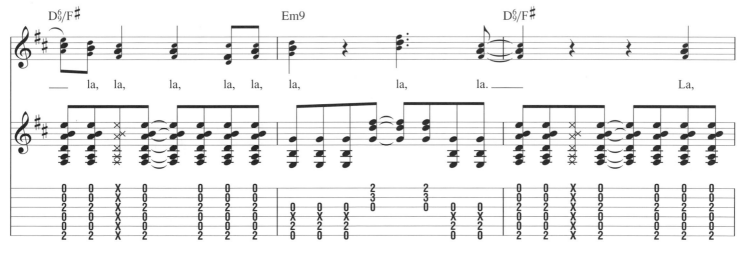

_ la,   la,   la,   la, la,   la,   la,   la. __   La,

Play 3 times & fade

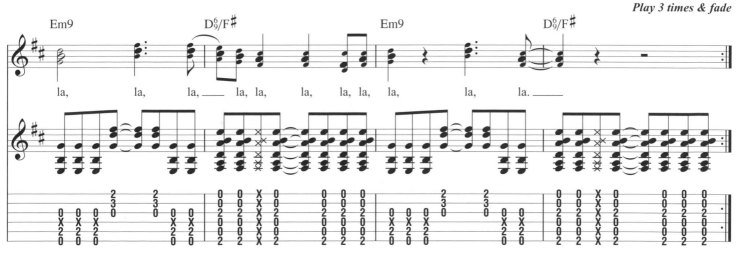

la,   la,   la, _ la, la,   la, la, la,   la,   la. __

Island in the Sun

Words and Music by Rivers Cuomo

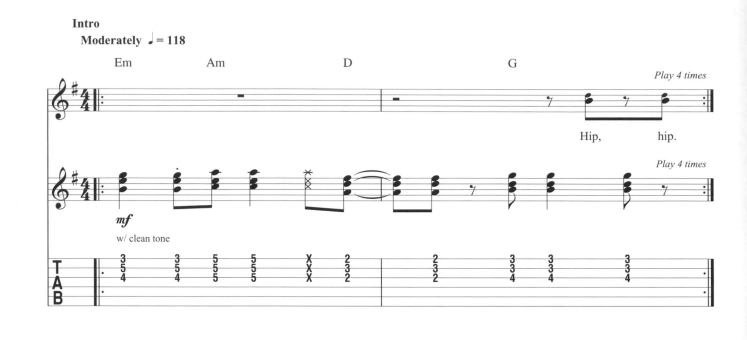

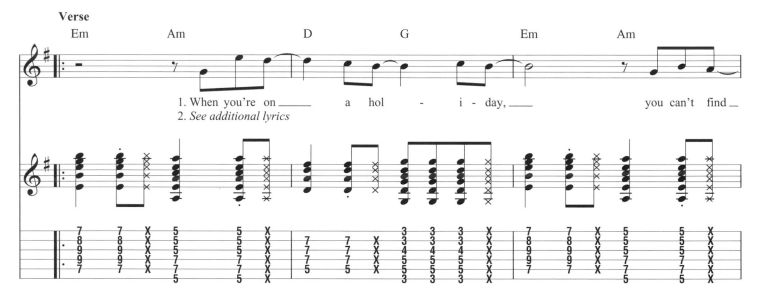

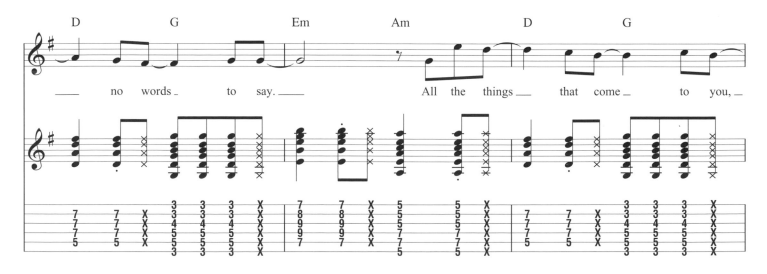

3rd time, substitute Fill 1

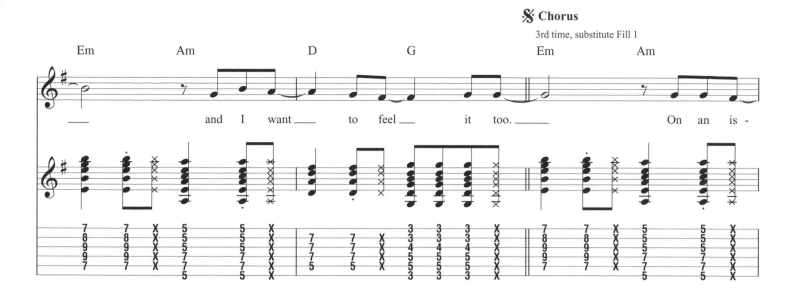

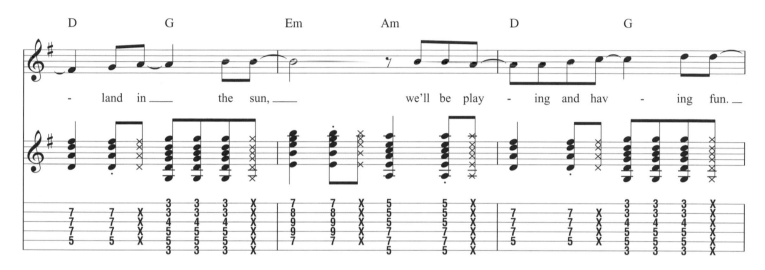

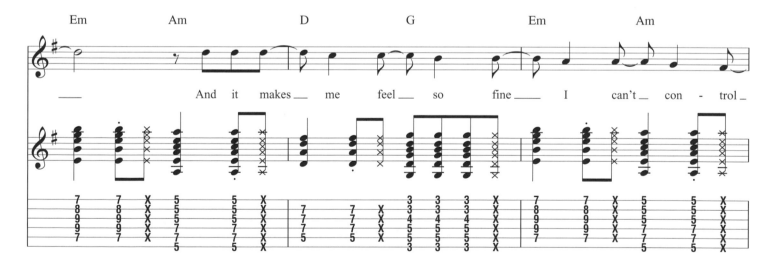

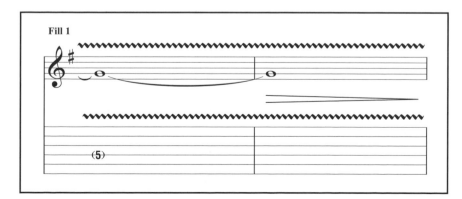

Fill 1

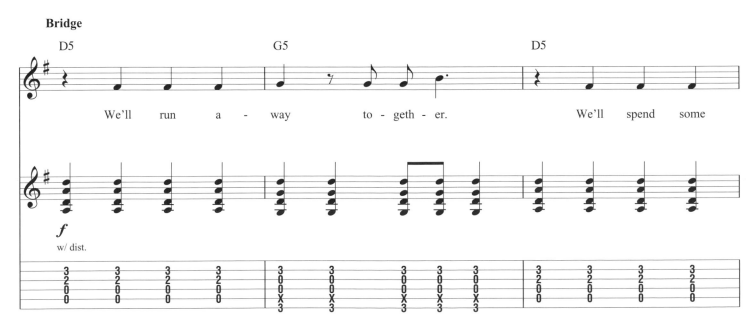

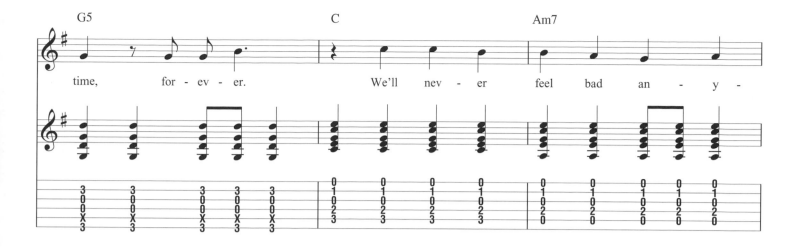

time, for - ev - er. We'll nev - er feel bad an - y -

To Coda ⊕

Interlude

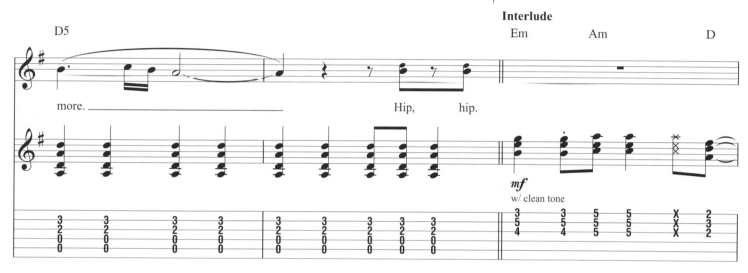

more. Hip, hip.

w/ clean tone

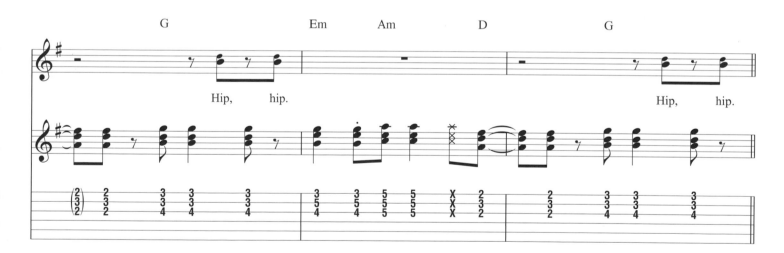

Hip, hip. Hip, hip.

Guitar Solo

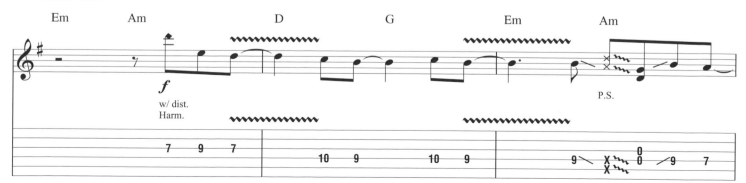

f
w/ dist.
Harm.

P.S.

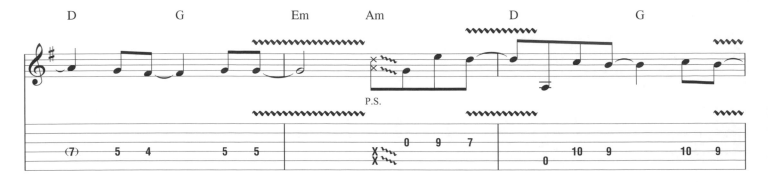

D.S. al Coda
(take 2nd ending)

Coda

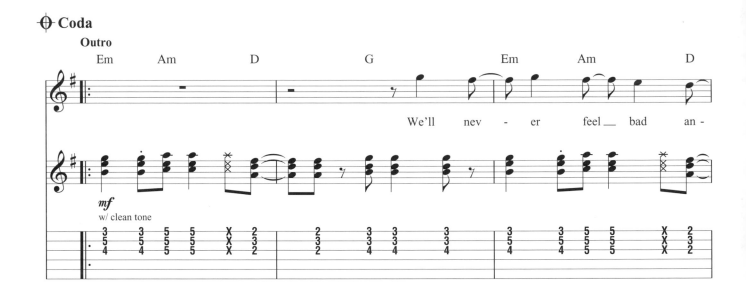

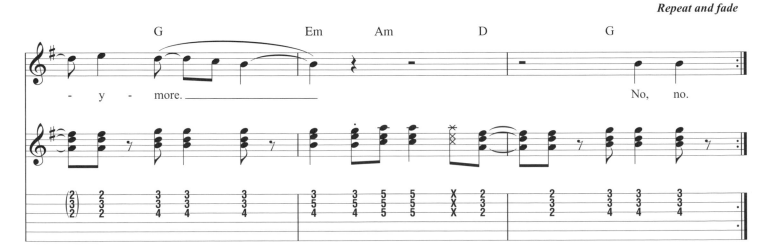

Additional Lyrics

2. When you're on a golden sea,
   You don't need no memory,
   Just a place to call your own
   As we drift into the zone.

One

Lyrics by Bono and The Edge
Music by U2

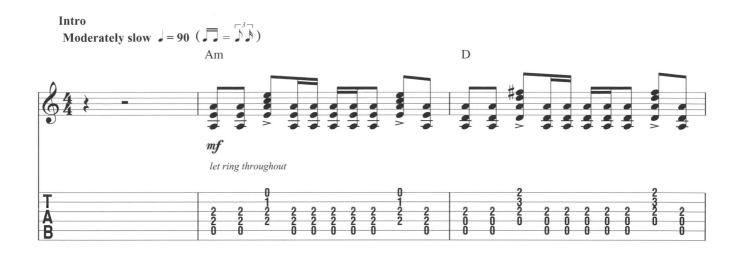

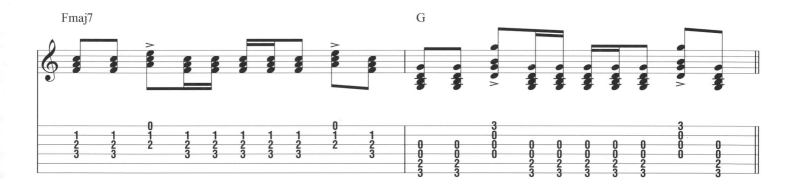

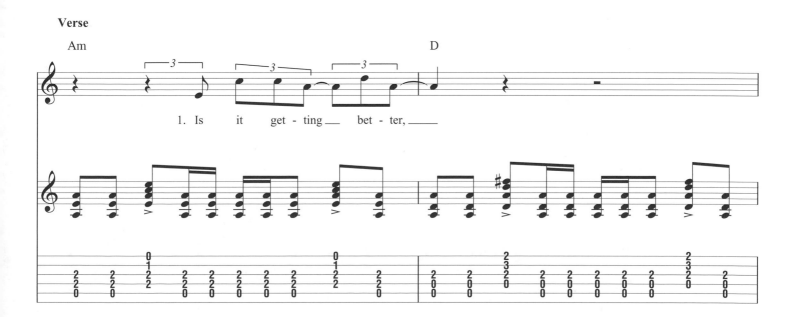

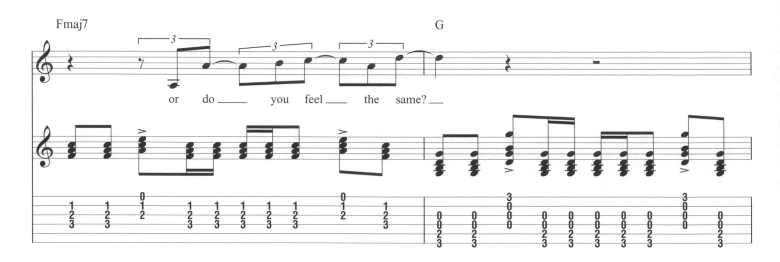

or do _____ you feel _____ the same? _____

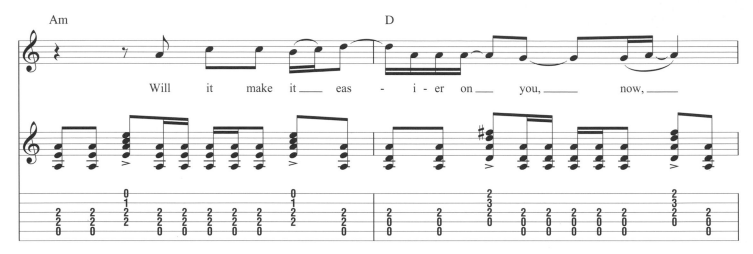

Will it make it _____ eas - i - er on _____ you, _____ now, _____

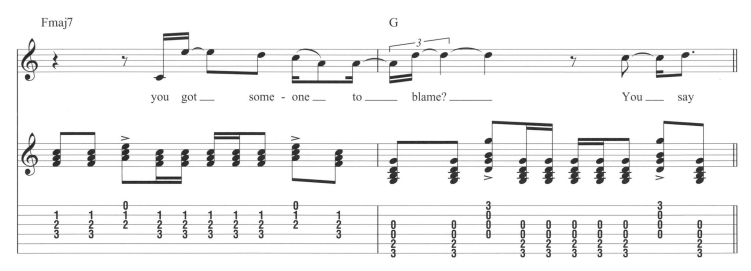

you got _____ some - one _____ to _____ blame? _____ You _____ say

Chorus

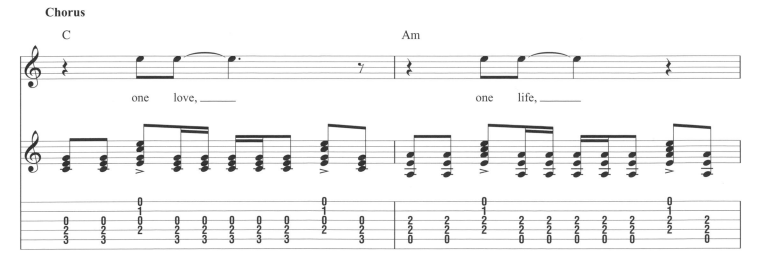

one love, _____ one life, _____

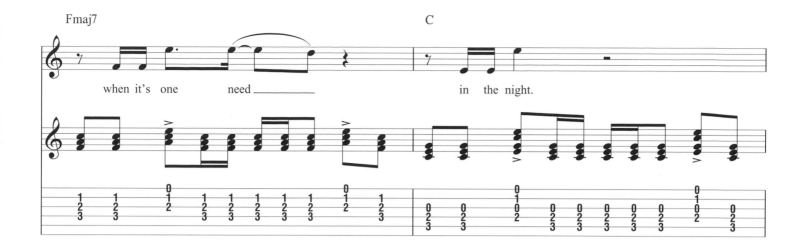

when it's one   need _____   in the night.

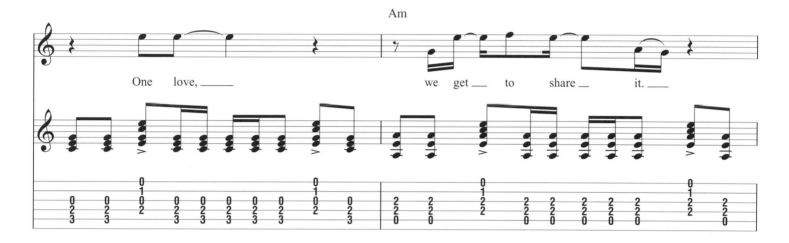

One   love, _____   we get __ to   share __   it. __

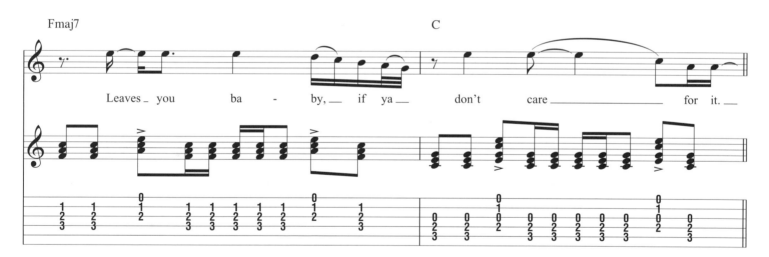

Leaves _ you   ba - by, __   if ya __   don't   care _____   for it. __

Interlude

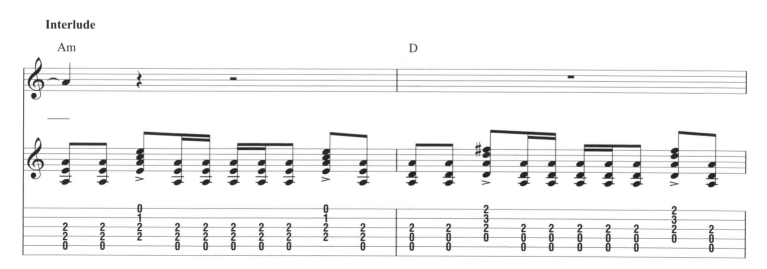

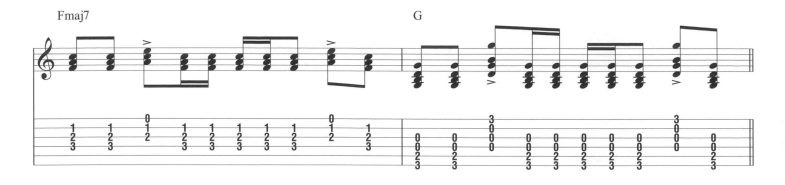

Verse

2. Did I dis - ap - point ____ you,
3. *See additional lyrics*

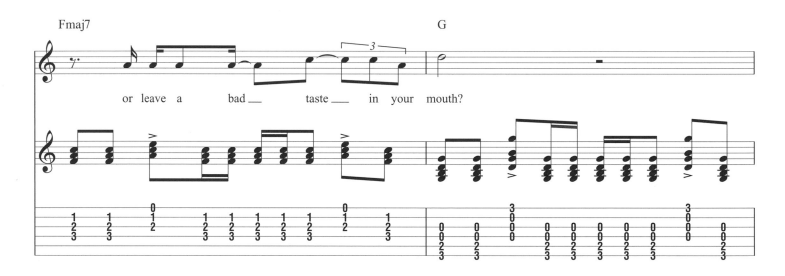

or leave a bad ___ taste ___ in your mouth?

You act ___ like you nev - er had love, ____

and you want me to go with-out.

Well, it's
See additional lyrics

Chorus

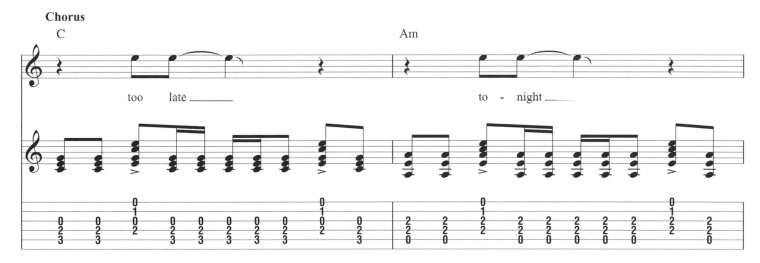

too late

to - night

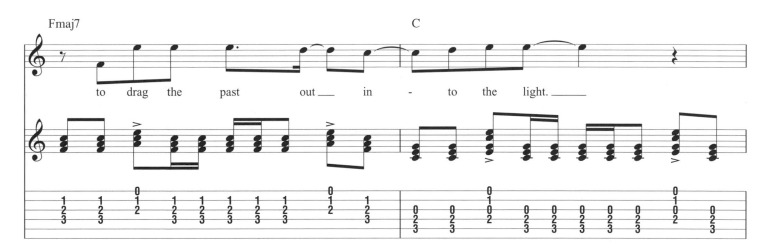

to drag the past out in - to the light.

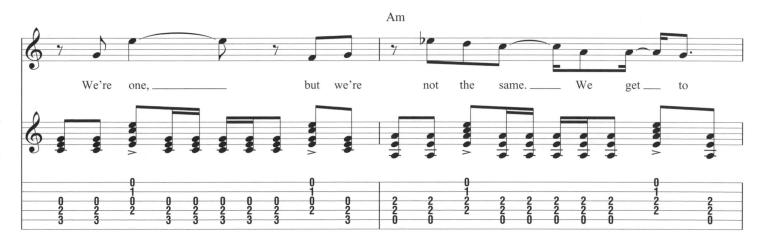

We're one, but we're not the same. We get to

89

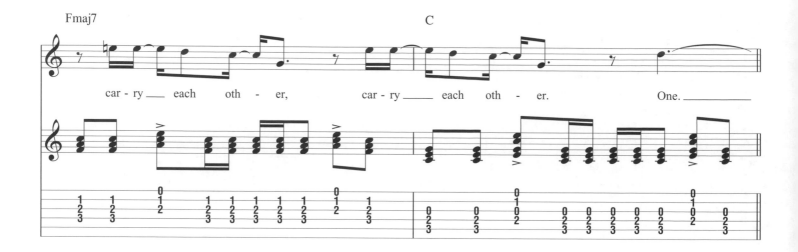

car - ry ___ each oth - er, car - ry ___ each oth - er. One. ___

1.

Interlude

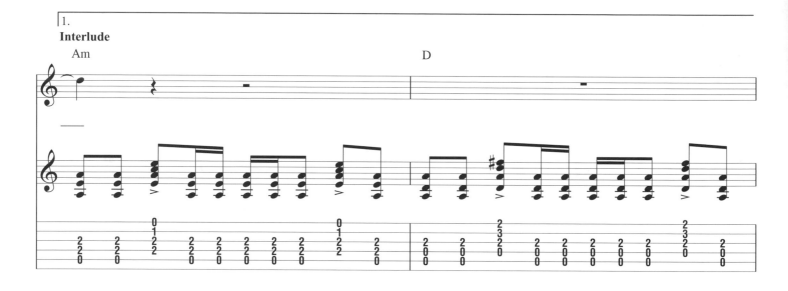

2.

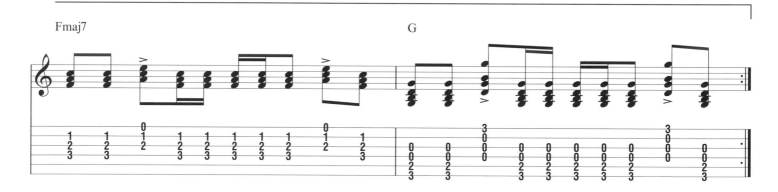

Bridge

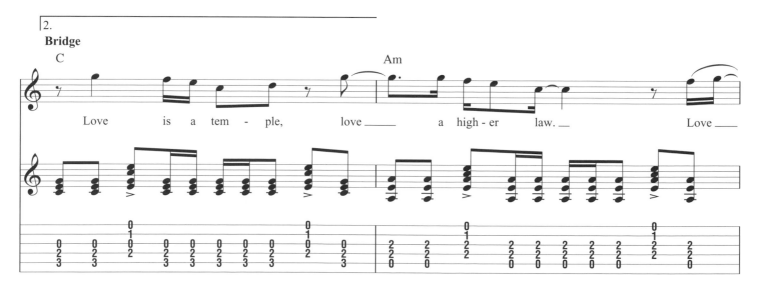

Love is a tem - ple, love ___ a high - er law. ___ Love ___

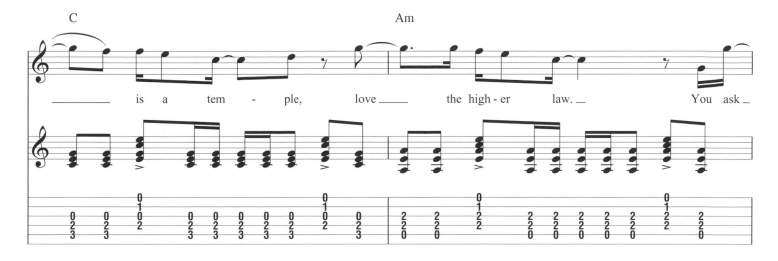

_____ is a tem - ple, love _____ the high - er law. _____ You ask _

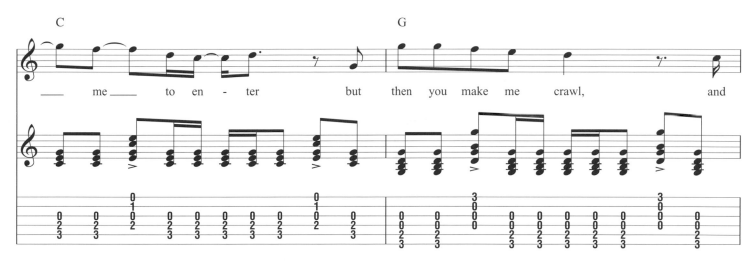

_____ me _____ to en - ter but then you make me crawl, _____ and

I can't _____ be hold - in' on _____ to what _ you've got, _____

Chorus

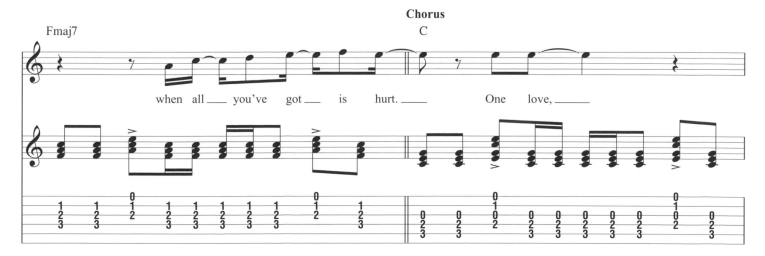

when all _____ you've got _____ is hurt. _____ One love, _____

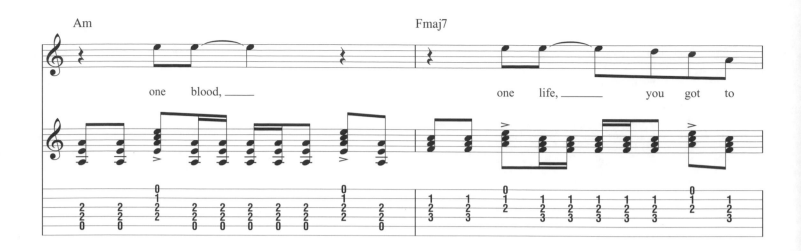

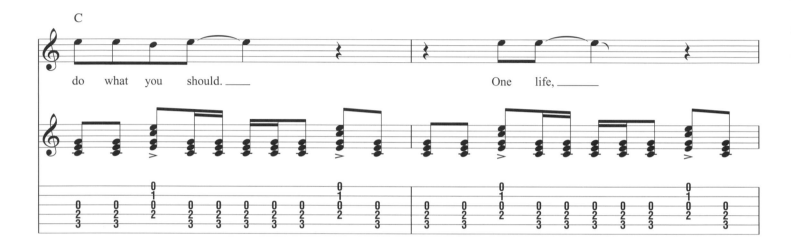

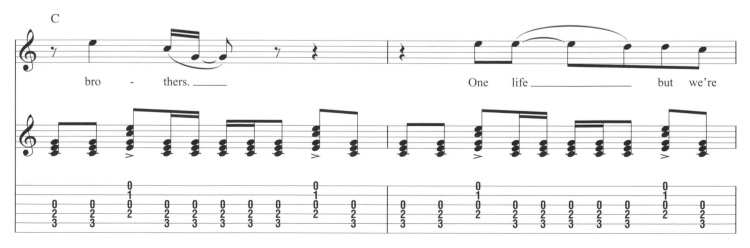

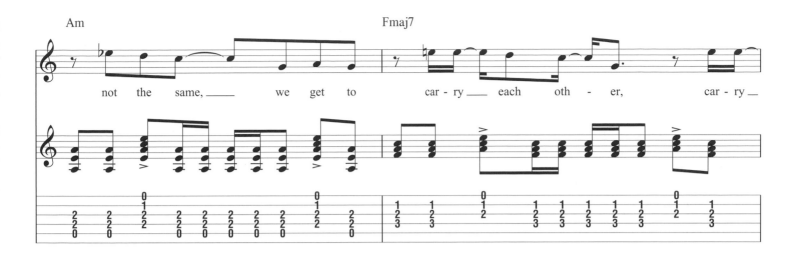

not the same, _____ we get to car - ry _____ each oth - er, car - ry _____

Outro

w/ Voc. ad lib. on repeats

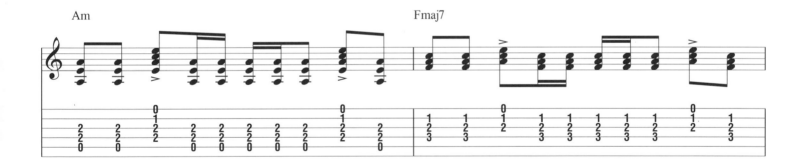

_____ each oth - er. One. _____

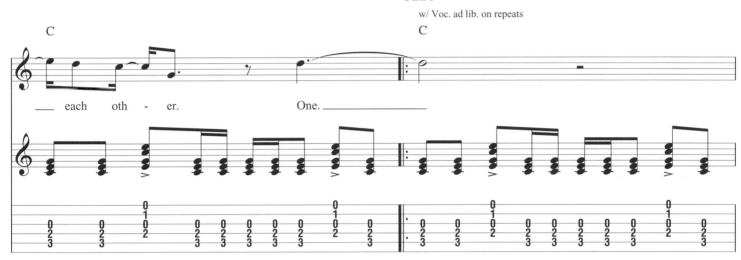

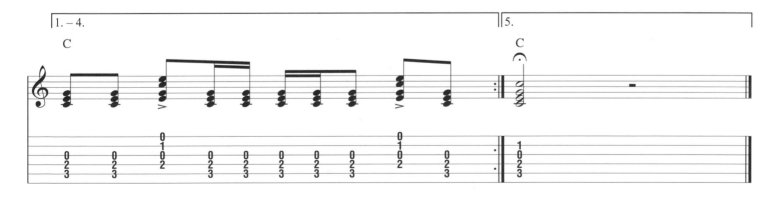

1. – 4.   5.

Additional Lyrics

3. Have you come here for forgiveness,
   Have you come to raise the dead?
   Have you come here to play Jesus,
   To the lepers in your head?

Chorus Did I ask too much? More than a lot?
         You gave me nothing, now it's all I got.
         We're one, but we're not the same.
         Well, we hurt each other, then we do it again.
         You say...

93

The Scientist

Words and Music by Guy Berryman, Jon Buckland, Will Champion and Chris Martin

*Symbols in parentheses represent chord names respective to capoed guitar.
Symbols above reflect actual sounding chords. Capoed fret is "0" in tab.

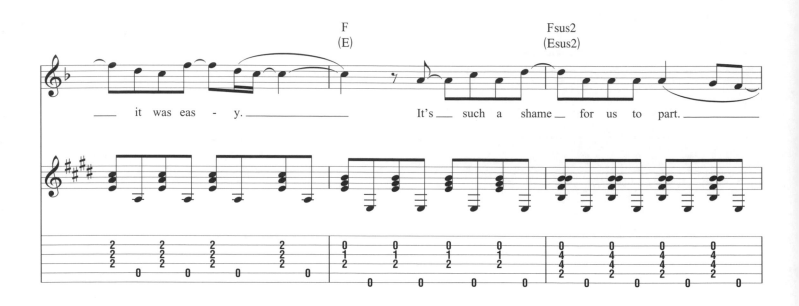

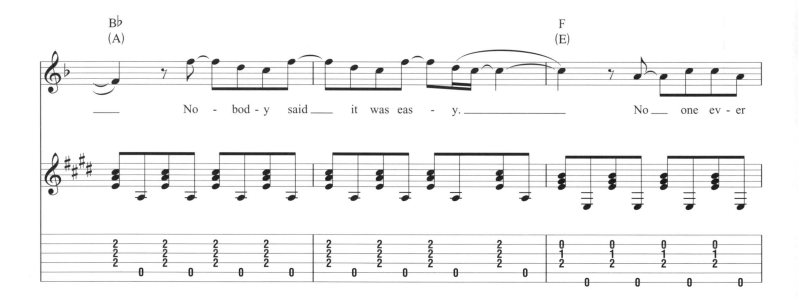

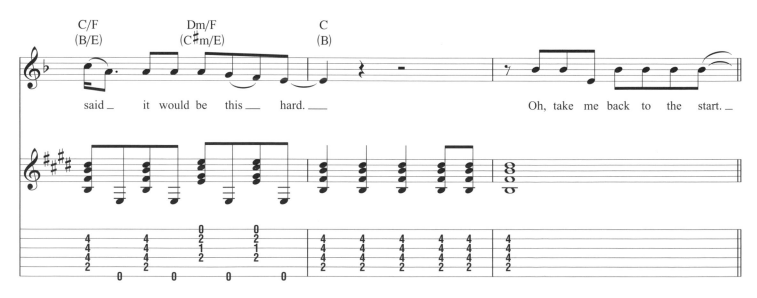

Interlude

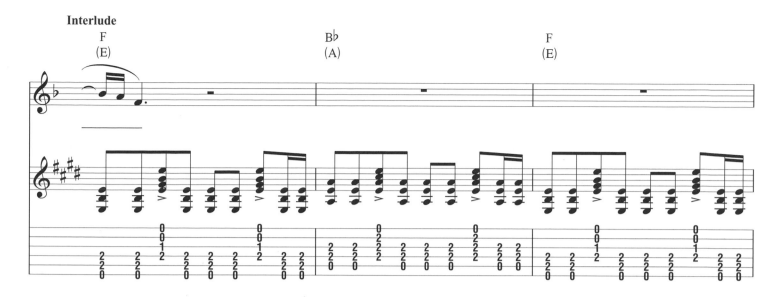

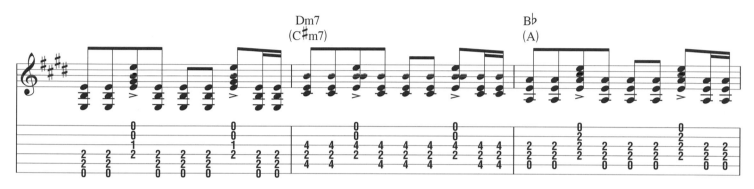

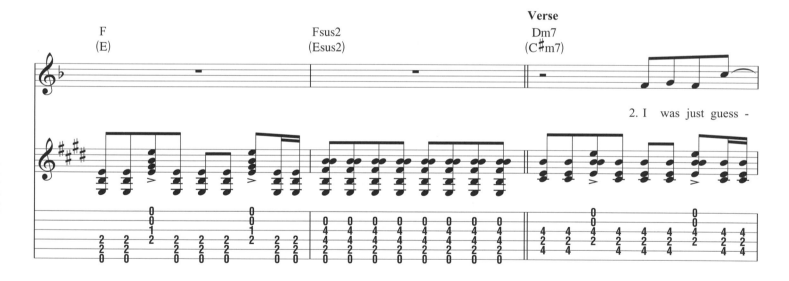

2. I was just guess-

-in' at num-bers and fig - ures, pull-ing your puz - zles a - part.

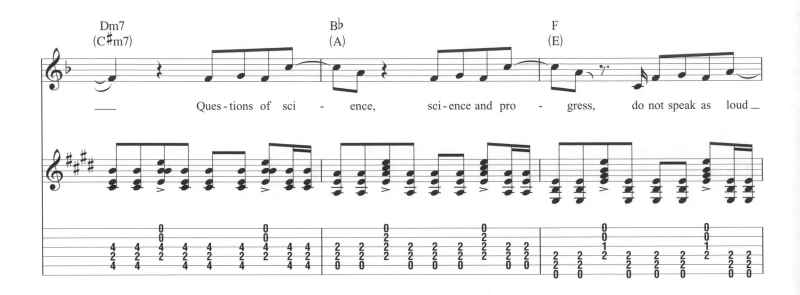

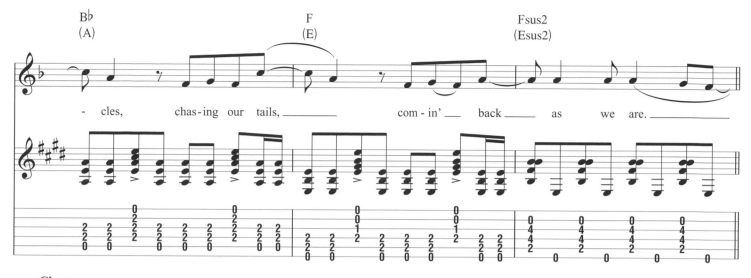

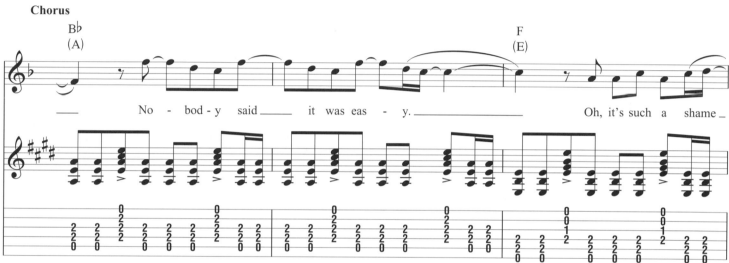

Chorus

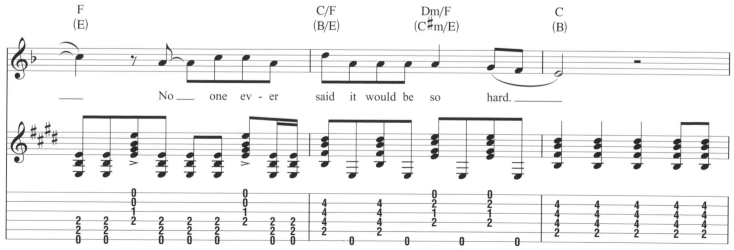

Interlude

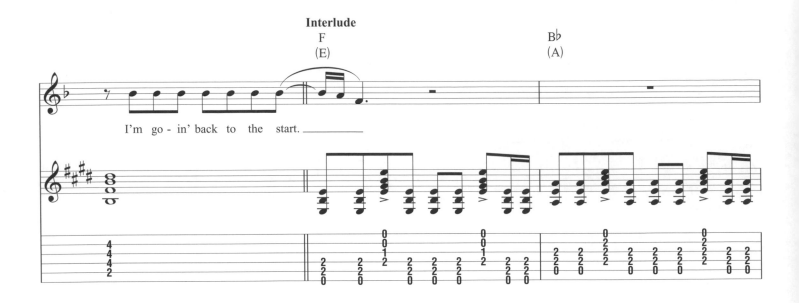

I'm go - in' back to the start. _____

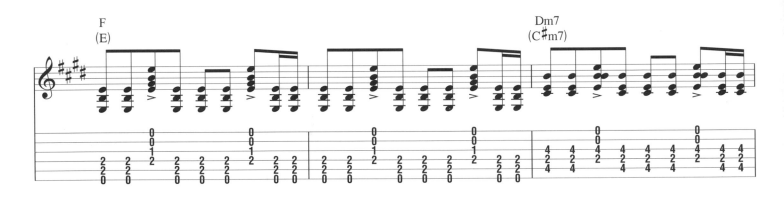

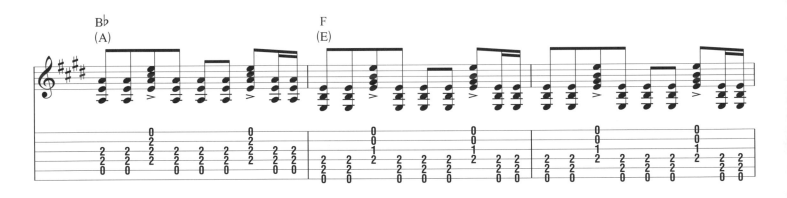

Outro

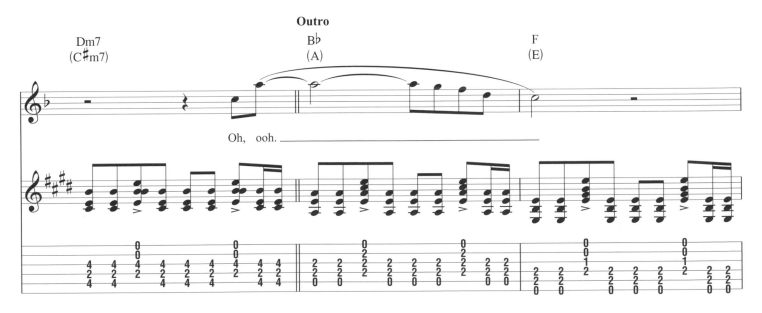

Oh, ooh. _____

Sunny Came Home

Words and Music by Shawn Colvin and John Leventhal

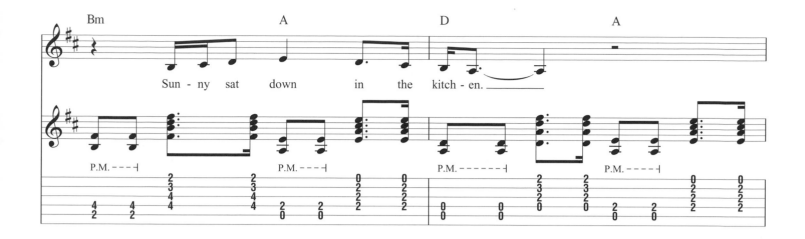

Sun - ny sat down in the kitch - en.

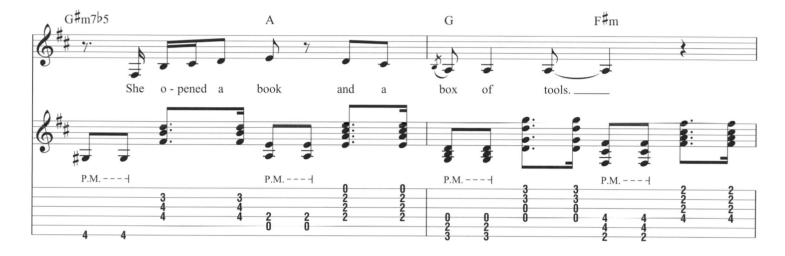

She o - pened a book and a box of tools.

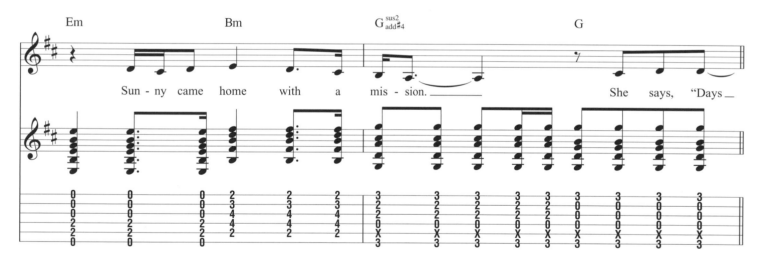

Sun - ny came home with a mis - sion. She says, "Days —

𝄋 **Chorus**

— go — by, I'm — hyp - no - tized. — I'm walk -

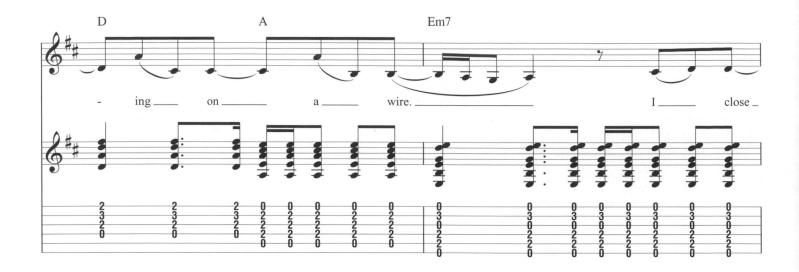

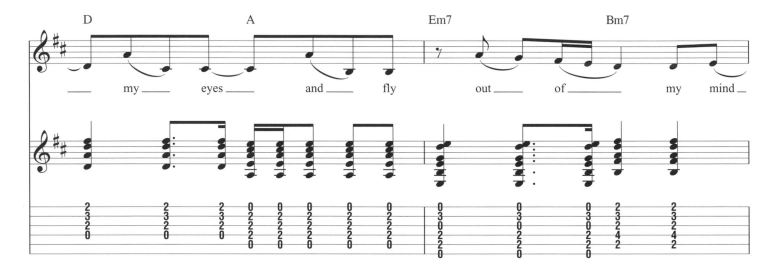

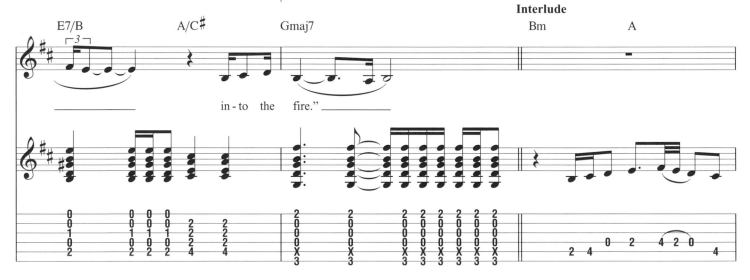

Verse

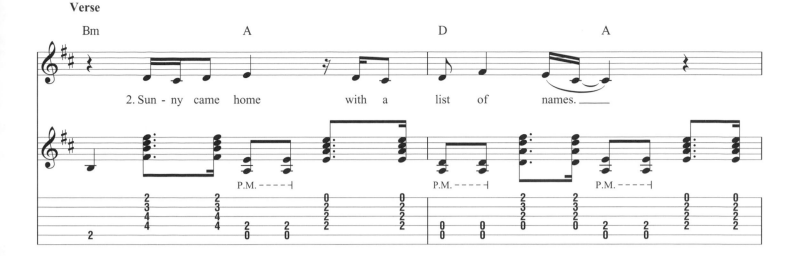

2. Sun-ny came home with a list of names.

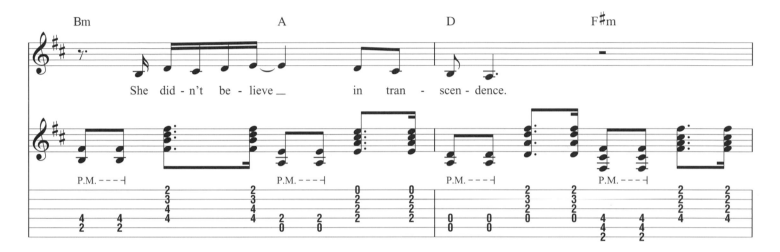

She did-n't be-lieve in tran-scen-dence.

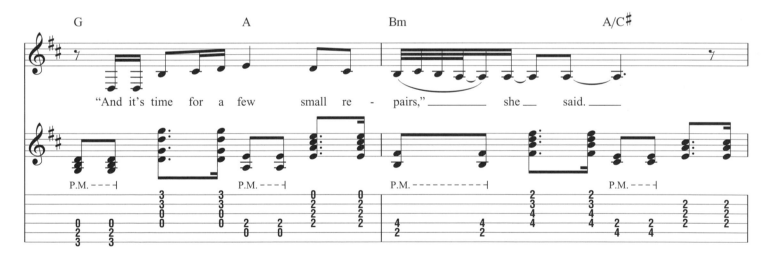

"And it's time for a few small re - pairs," she said.

D.S. al Coda

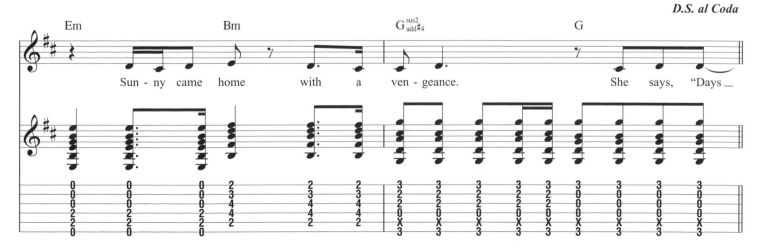

Sun-ny came home with a ven-geance. She says, "Days

⊕ Coda

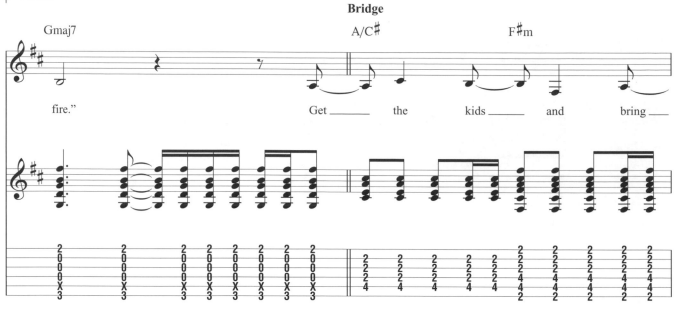

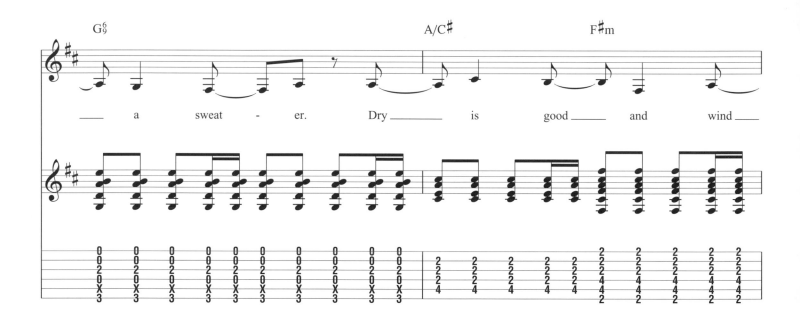

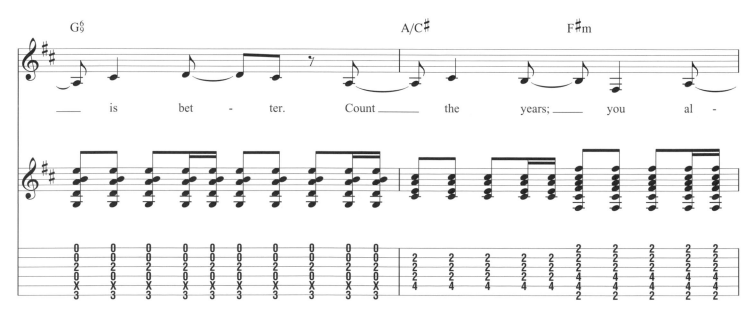

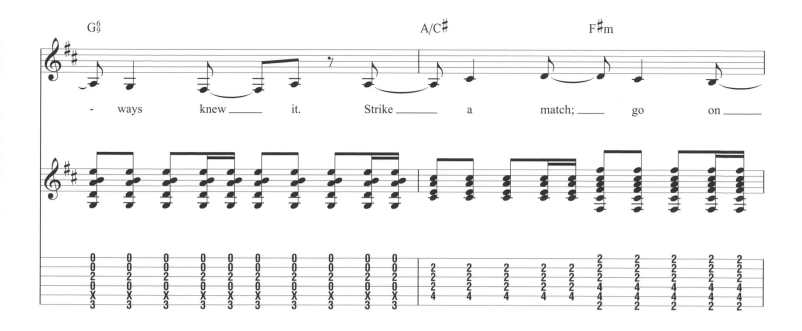

Chorus

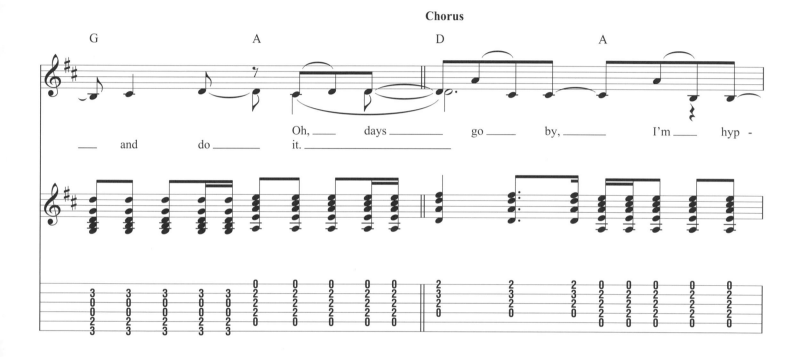

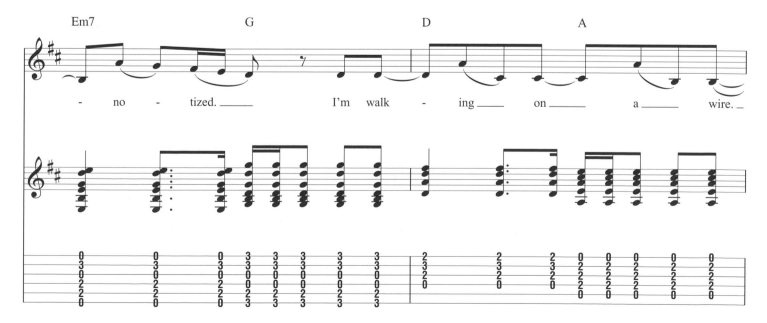

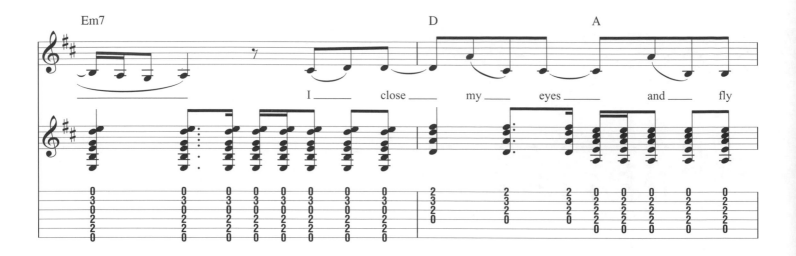

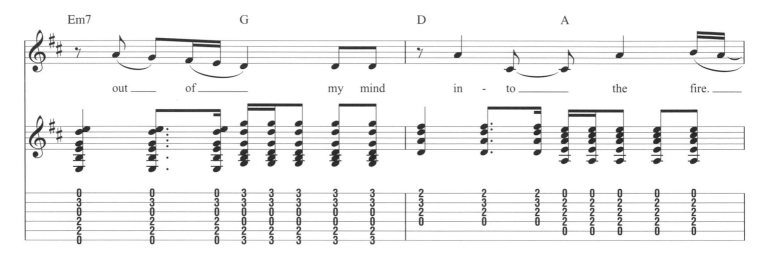

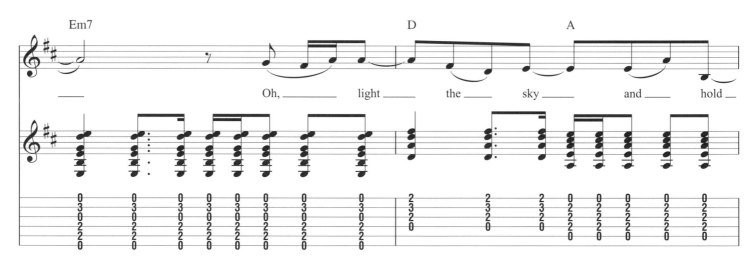

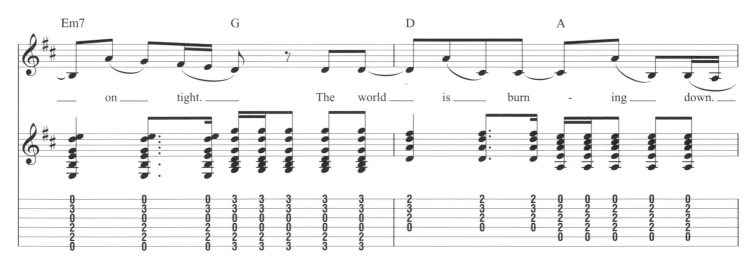

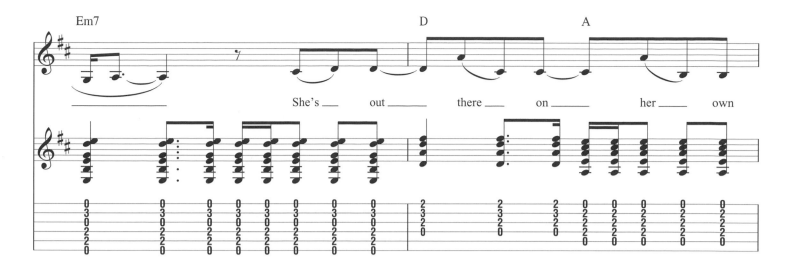

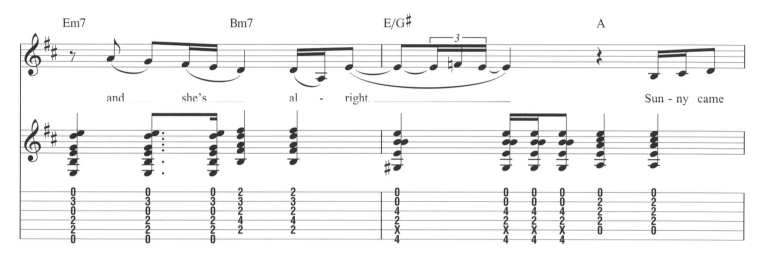

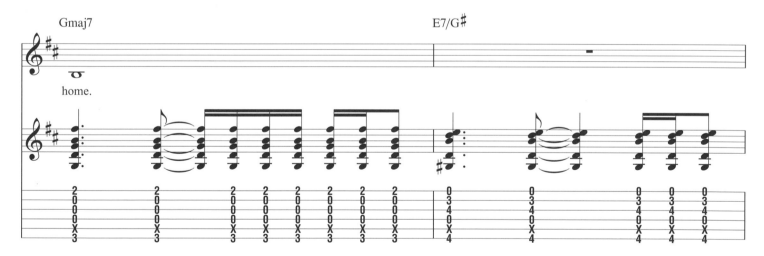

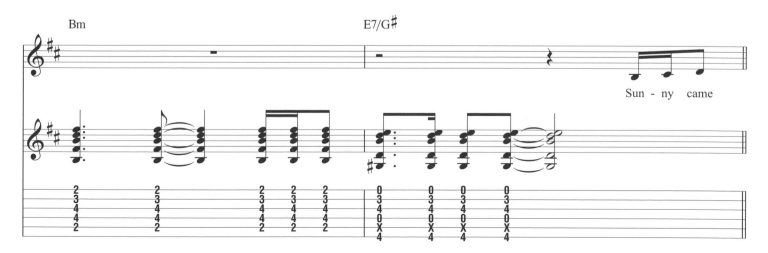

Outro

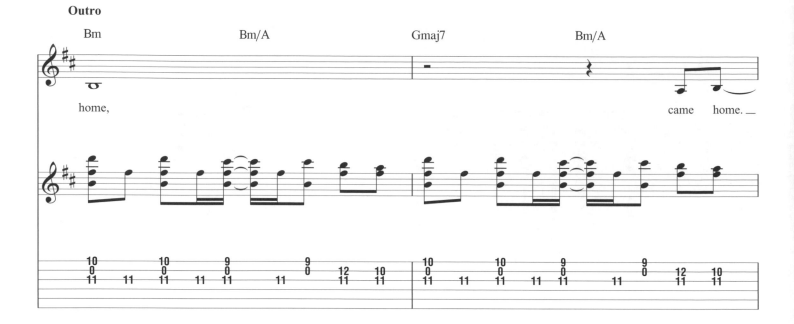

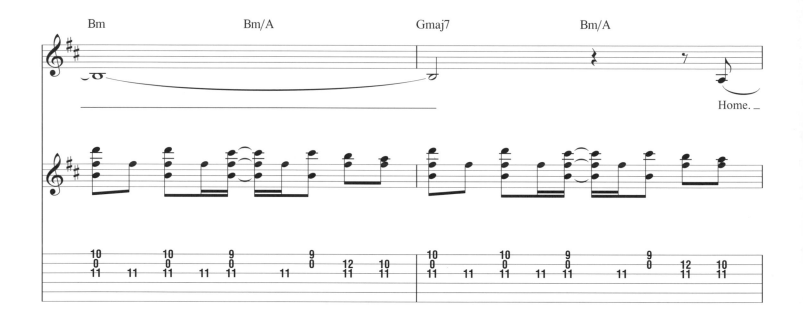

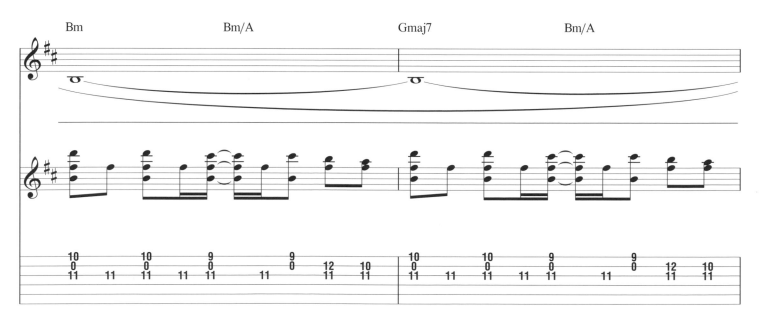

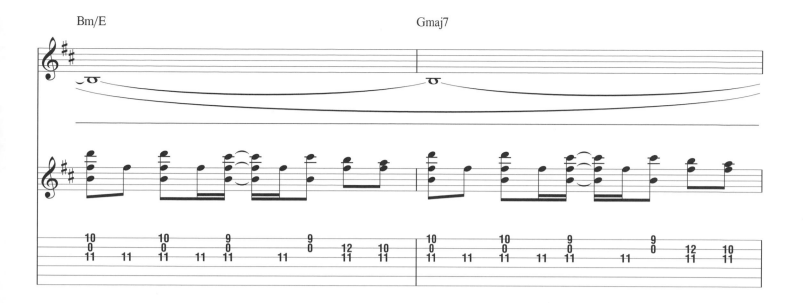

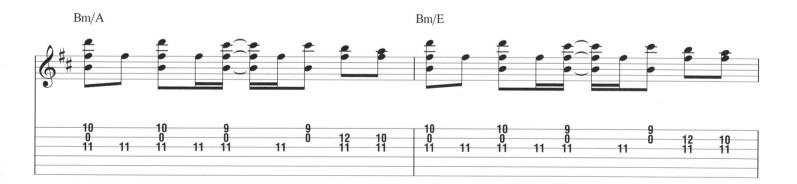

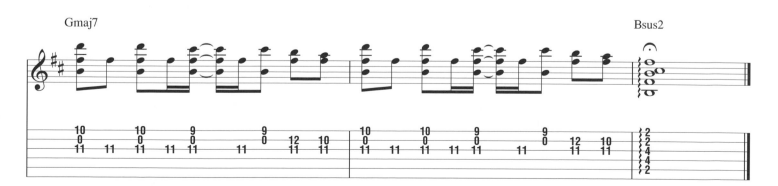

What's Up

Words and Music by Linda Perry

Intro
Slow ♩ = 67

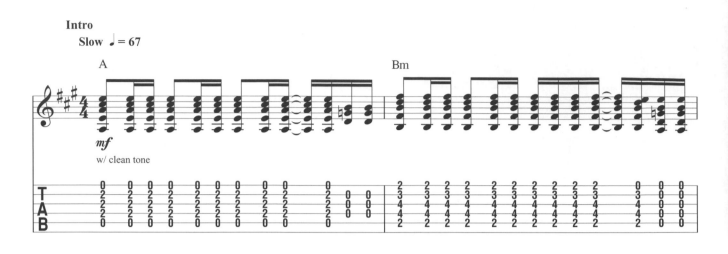

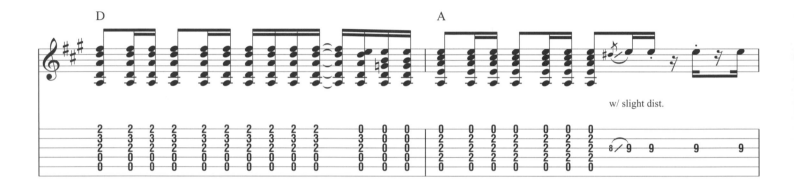

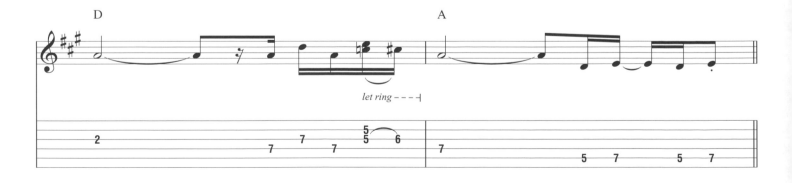

Verse

1. Twen-ty five years and my life is still ___ try'n' to get up ___ that great big hill ___ of ___ hope ___

dist. off

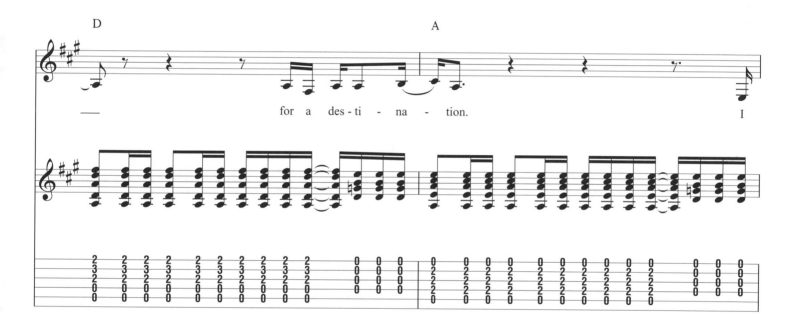

___ Twen-ty five years and my life is still ___ try'n' to get up ___ that ___ for a des-ti - na - tion. I

real-ized quick - ly when I knew I should, ___ that the world ___ was made up of this broth-er - hood ___ of ___ man, ___

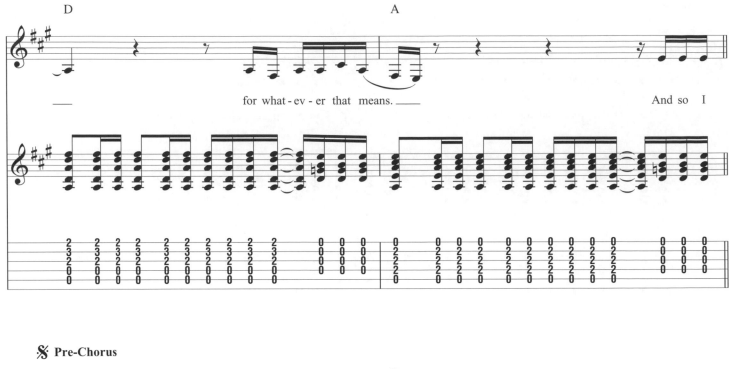

for what - ev - er that means. ___ And so I

𝄇 Pre-Chorus

cry ___ some - times when I'm ly - ing in bed ___ just to get it all out, ___ what's in ___ my head, ___ and I, ___

I am feel - ing a lit - tle pe - cu - liar. And so I

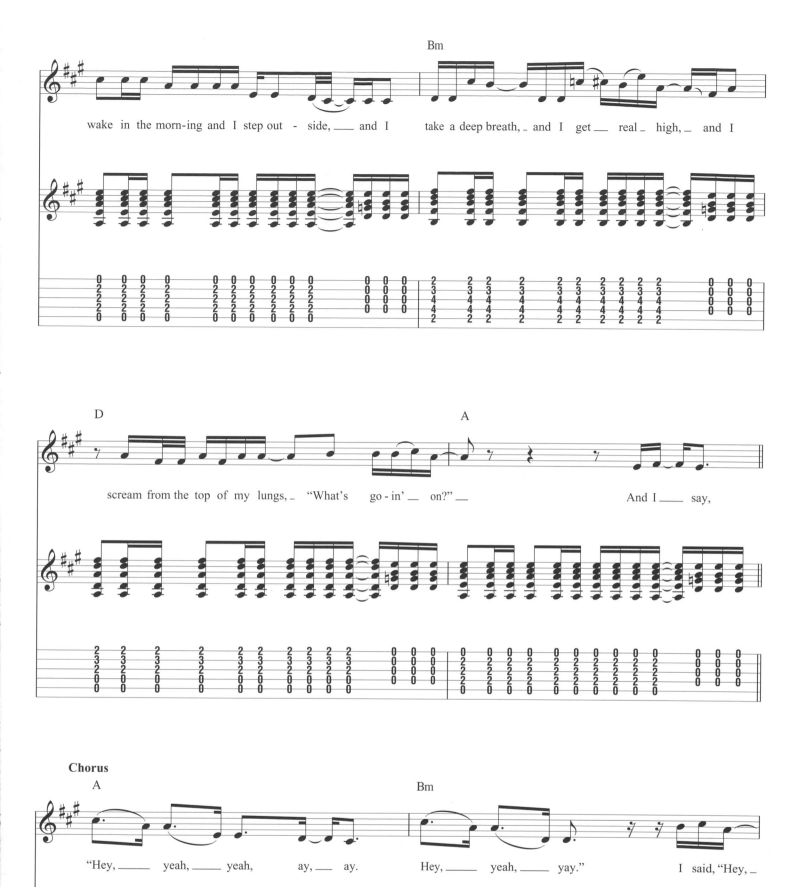

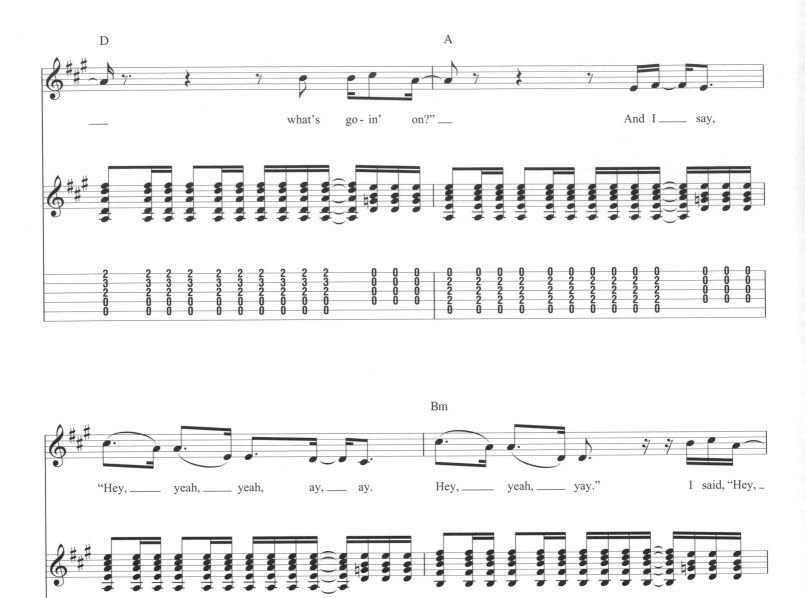

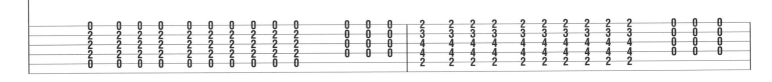

Interlude

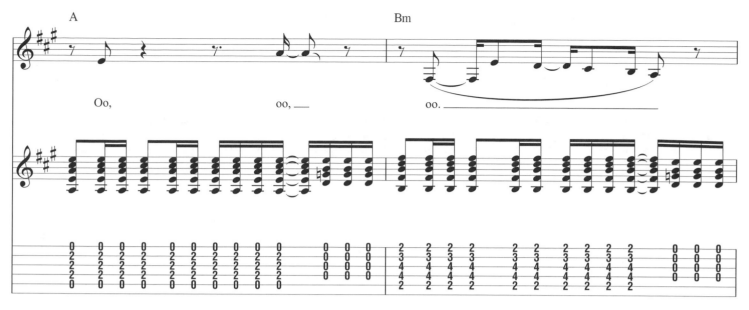

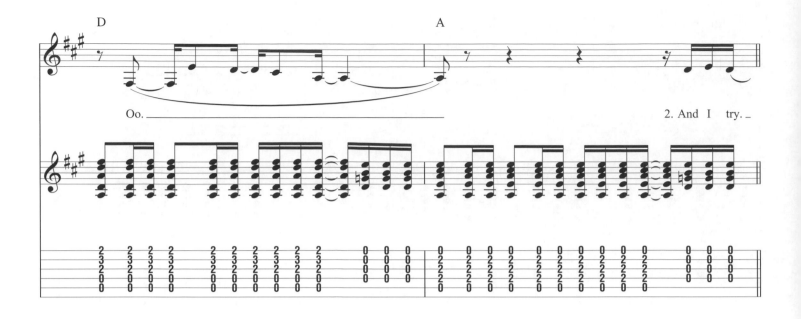

Verse

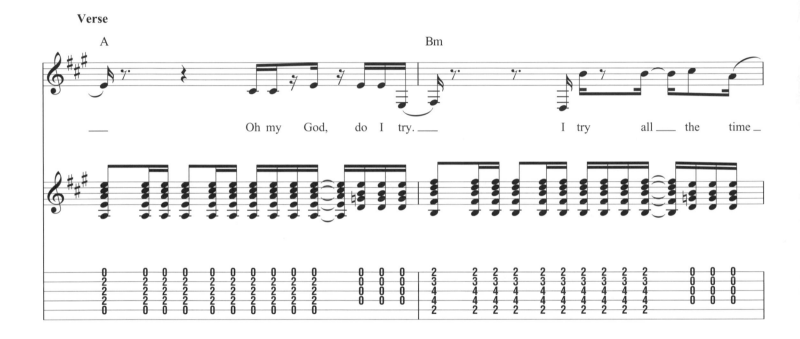

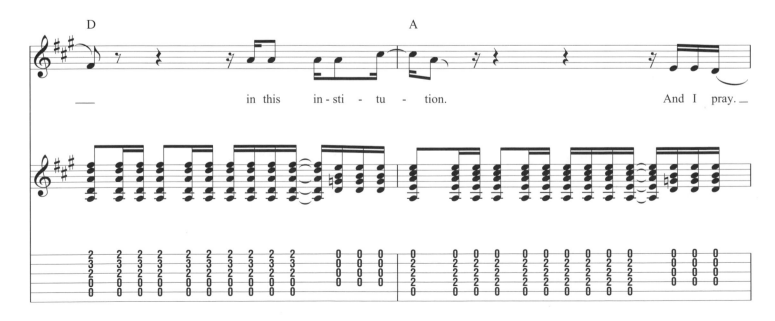

Oh my God, do I pray. ___ I pray ev-'ry sin - gle day ___

D.S. al Coda

for a rev-o - lu - tion. ___ And so I

𝄏 **Coda**

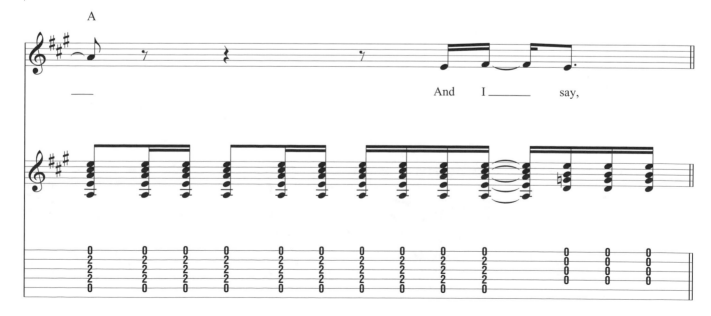

And I ___ say,

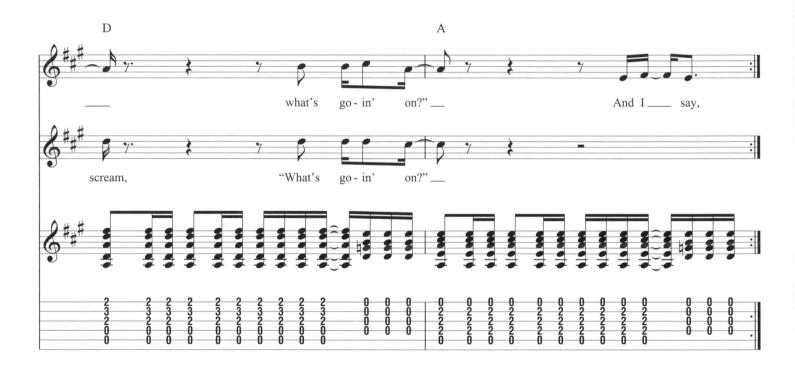

Outro

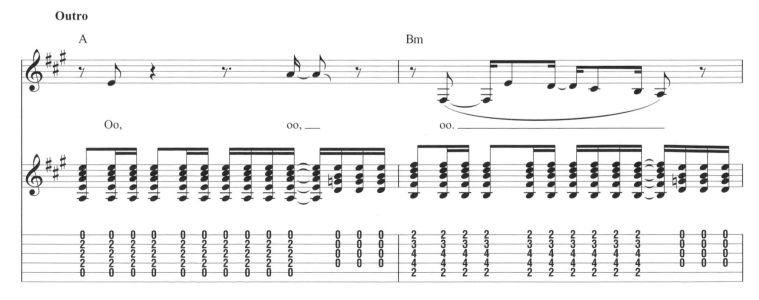

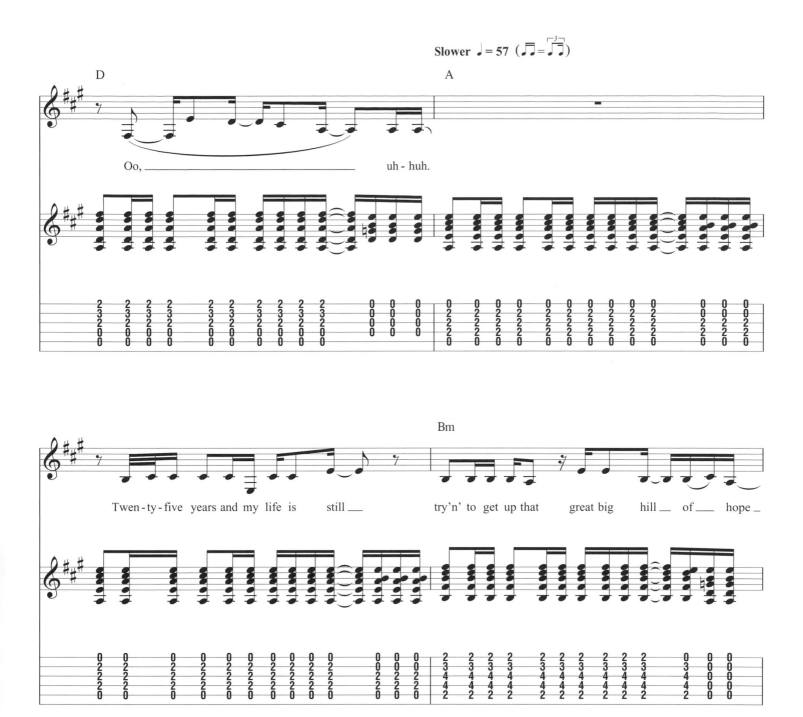

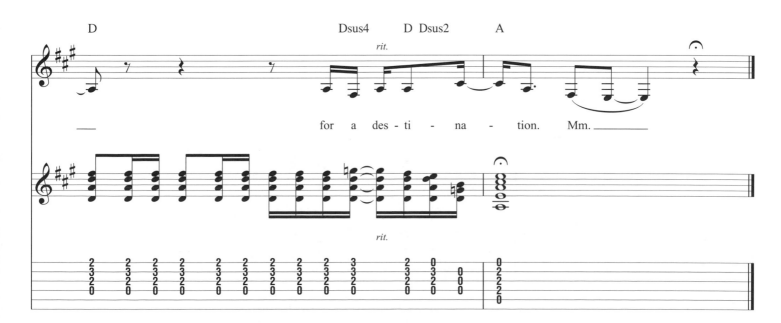

Redemption Song

Words and Music by Bob Marley

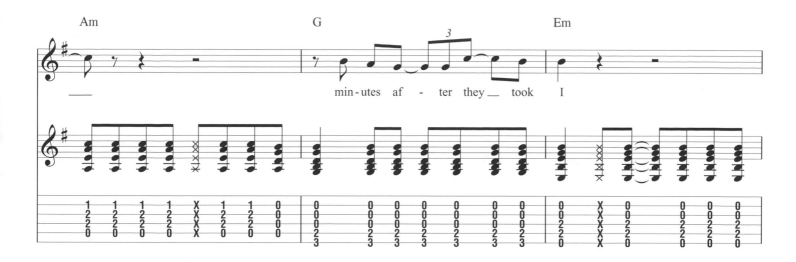

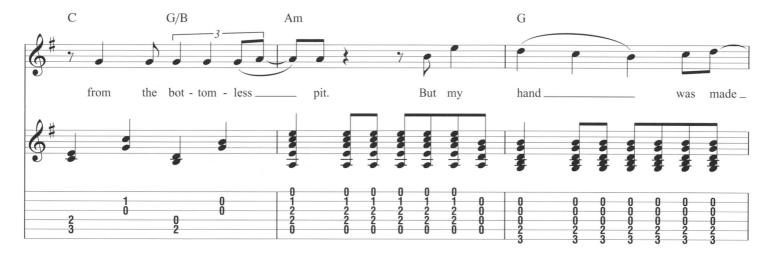

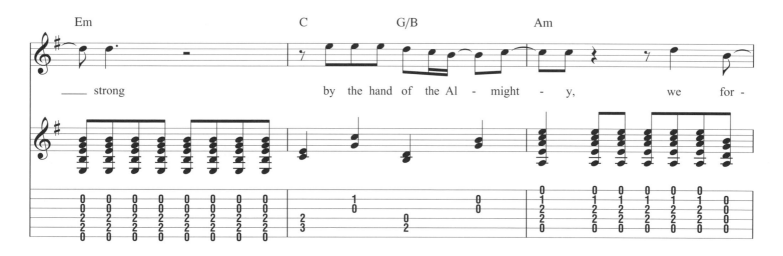

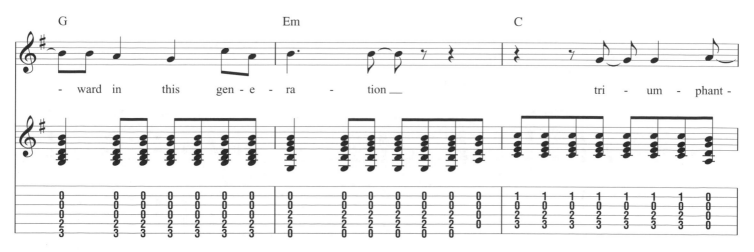

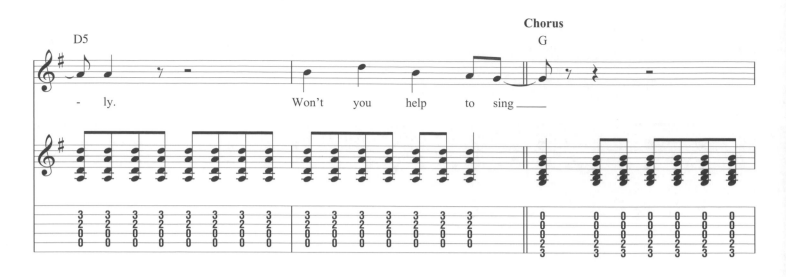

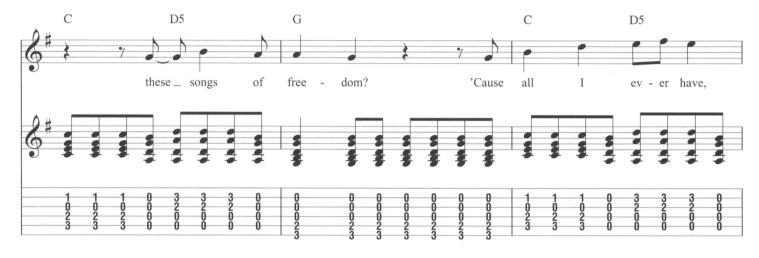

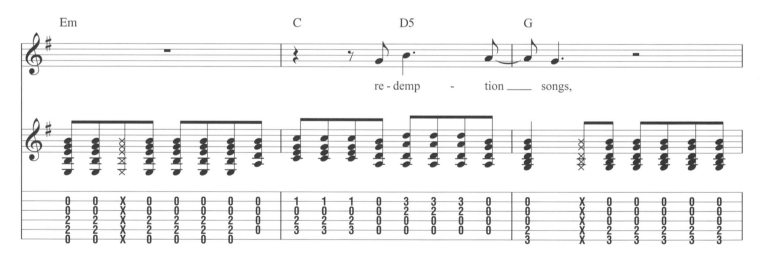

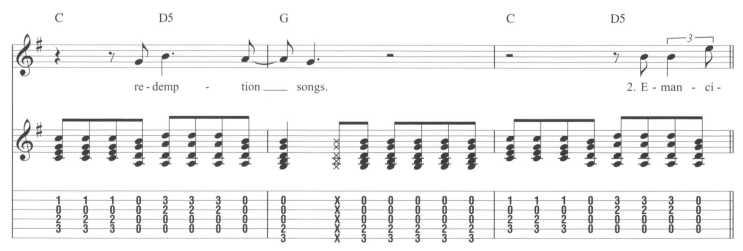

𝄋 Verse

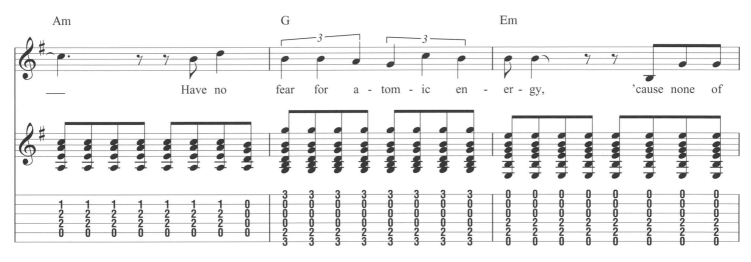

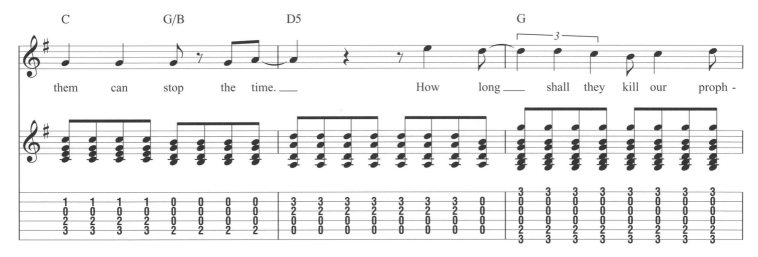

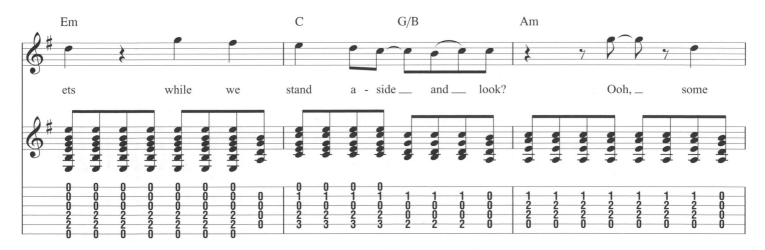

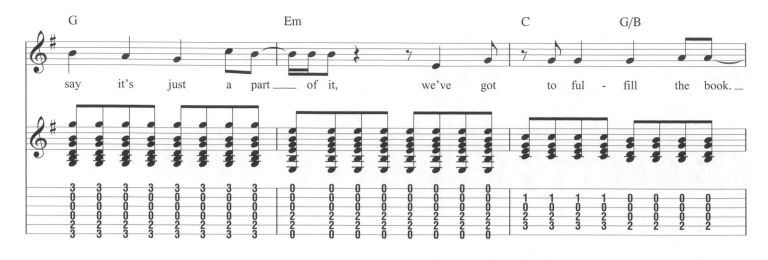

say it's just a part ___ of it, we've got to ful - fill the book. __

Chorus

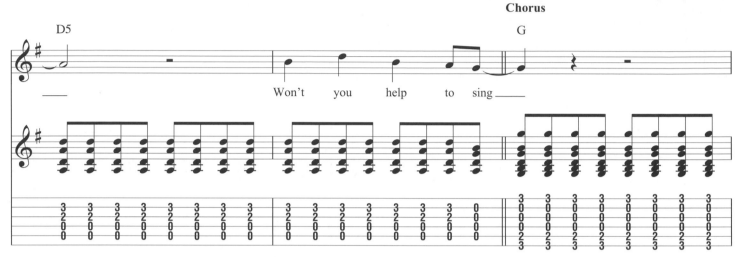

__ Won't you help to sing __

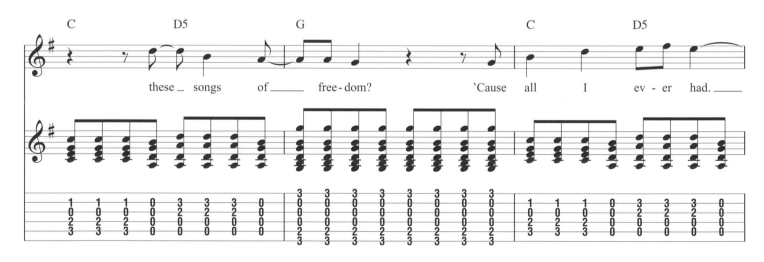

these _ songs of __ free-dom? 'Cause all I ev - er had. __

To Coda ⊕

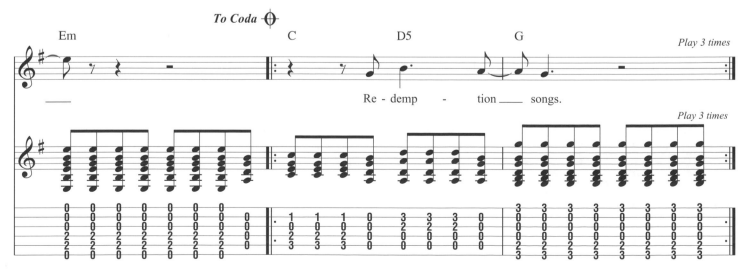

__ Re - demp - tion __ songs.

Play 3 times

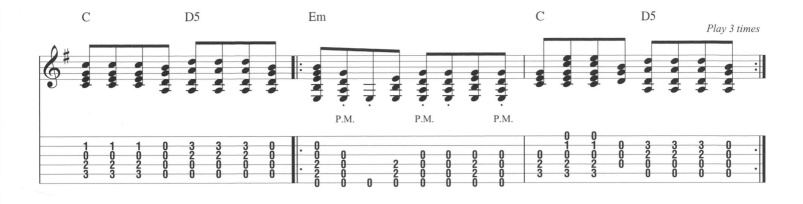

D.S. al Coda

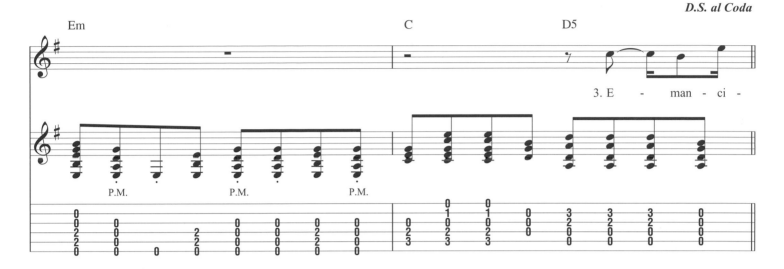

3. E - man - ci -

Coda

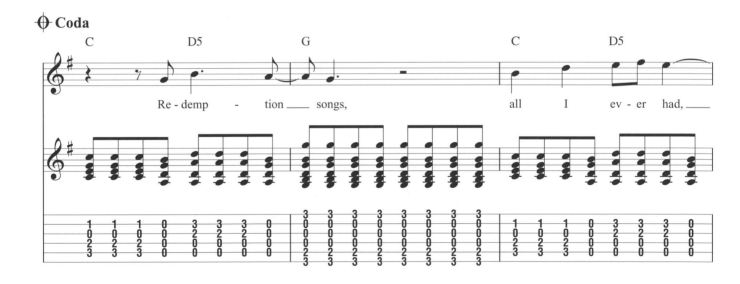

Re - demp - tion ___ songs, all I ev - er had, ___

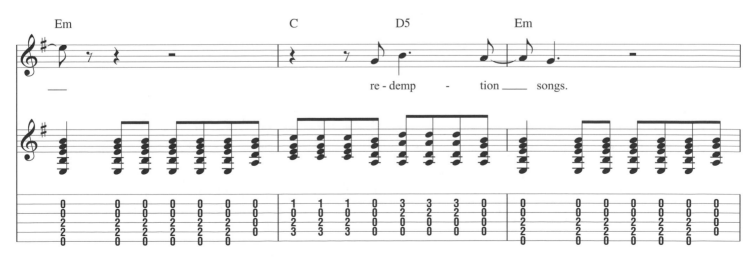

___ re - demp - tion ___ songs.

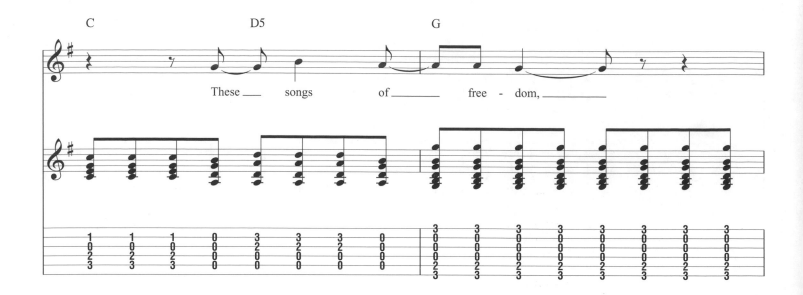

These ___ songs of _____ free - dom, _____

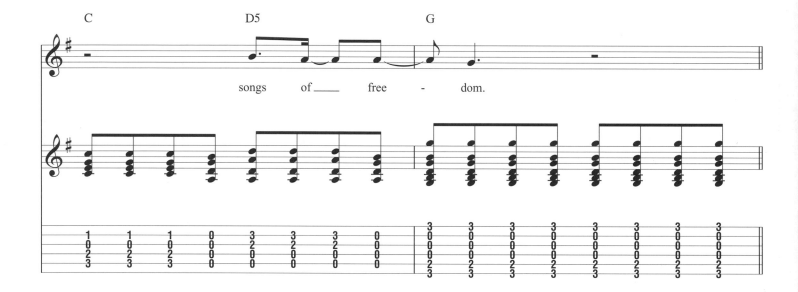

songs of ___ free - dom.

Outro

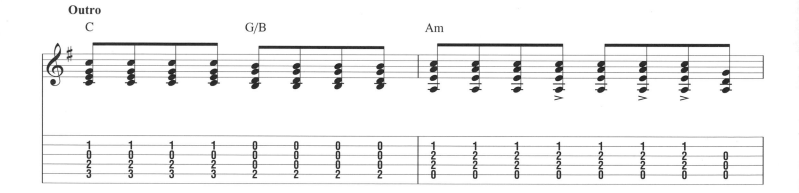

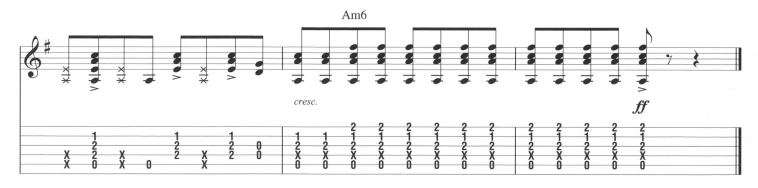